The Big Book of

Icebreakers

The Big Book of
Icebreakers

50 Quick, Fun Activities for Energizing Meetings and Workshops

Edie West

McGraw-Hill

New York   San Francisco   Washington, D.C.   Auckland   Bogotá
Caracas   Lisbon   London   Madrid   Mexico City   Milan
Montreal   New Delhi   San Juan   Singapore
Sydney   Tokyo   Toronto

McGraw-Hill

A Division of The **McGraw·Hill** Companies

Portions of this book were previously published in *201 Icebreakers* by Edie West.

          3 4 5 6 7 8 9 0   ACG / ACG   0 9 8 7 6 5 4 3 2 1 0

ISBN 0-07-134984-7

The sponsoring editor for this book was Richard Narramore, the editing supervisor was Fred Dahl, and the production supervisor was Modestine Cameron. It was set in Gill Sans by Inkwell Publishing Services.

Printed and bound by Arcata Graphics.

McGraw-Hill books are available at special quantity discounts to use as premiums and sales promotions, or for use in corporate training programs. For more information, please write to the Director of Special Sales, McGraw-Hill, Two Penn Plaza, New York, NY 10121-2298. Or contact your local bookstore.

 This book is printed on recycled, acid-free paper containing a minimum of 50% recycled de-inked fiber.

Contents

Icebreakers for Groups of 20 or More   61

Icebreakers for Team Building   79

Icebreakers for Pure Fun   97

Icebreakers for Introducing a Topic   113

Icebreakers for Outdoors   133

Icebreakers for Self-Disclosure 151

Icebreakers for Stuffy, Conservative Types Who Hate Icebreakers 171

Icebreakers While Waiting to Start 185

Icebreakers for Everyday Living 201

Icebreakers for the Super Intelligent 217

Acknowledgments

Many thanks to: Richard Narramore, for suggesting I write this book; Ron Greene, my son, for formatting, editing, and encouraging; Glenn West, my husband, for listening, laughing, encouraging, and supporting; and a special thanks to God, for the gifts of family, friends, and fun.

Edie West

Introduction

Icebreakers occur rather naturally in the workplace all the time. Employees begin staff meetings by relating a humorous anecdote or telling a personal story. People plan celebrations for birthdays, retirements, congratulations, or accomplishment. Icebreakers are important because they add emotional value to a situation, meeting, or presentation. They're never a necessity, but always needed. Icebreakers encourage self-disclosure, humor, respect for others and their opinions, thought, and creativity. They provide an escape valve for tension from daily interactions. Most importantly, they allow people to laugh at themselves.

Important Messages in an Icebreaker

Icebreakers send metaphorical messages for healthful living. Here are some of the messages contained in this book of icebreakers:

Icebreakers for Staff Meetings. Staff meetings can be places for laughter, creativity, self-disclosure, appreciation, and enjoyment of one another.

Icebreakers for Sales Meetings. Sales meetings can be full of energy, laughter, creativity, challenge, and achievement.

Icebreakers for Complete Strangers. You can laugh with, learn to appreciate, and get to know complete strangers quickly and in a nonthreatening way.

Icebreakers for Groups of 20 or More. You can quickly get to know other people in a large group setting. It is easy to have fun and be creative in a large group; large groups bring a great deal of energy into a setting.

Icebreakers for Team Building. Interdependency is valuable for all involved. Being part of a team opens the door to successes one would not be able to experience alone. I value my team members and they value me.

Icebreakers for Pure Fun. Pure fun is physically healthful.

Icebreakers for Introducing a Topic. It is always helpful to look at a topic in a fresh way.

Icebreakers for Outdoors. Physical activity can build positive interactions.

Icebreakers for Self-Disclosure. People can reveal information that increases the level of understanding between them.

Icebreakers for Stuffy, Conservative Types Who Hate Icebreakers. It's okay to let down your defenses and interact with others.

Tips for Facilitators

Anyone can use icebreakers, but using them successfully requires practice and skill. Practice allows the leader to experience enough success to be confident in the choice and appropriate use of icebreakers. Gaining skill means increasing the enjoyment of your delivery—changing activities to experiences.

There is no hard and fast rule about when to use an icebreaker, but being sure they have the best use involves planning, at least at first. When planning to use an icebreaker, ask yourself these questions:

Why am I thinking about using an icebreaker? In other words, what value would an icebreaker add to this situation?

What would be the result if I didn't use an icebreaker?

What icebreaker would create the experience needed?

How will this group of people react to this icebreaker?

How should I introduce it, facilitate it, and close it?

How will I know if it's been successful? (Go back to #1.)

What's the worst that could happen if I use an icebreaker, and how would I deal with it?

Opening and Closing Lines for Icebreakers

The success of an icebreaker may depend on the introduction or closure. Here are some opening and closing lines that have been successful for me.

Opening. . .

"Since we don't know one another, I thought it might be helpful to take a few minutes to find out something about each other."

"Since we will soon be leaving for a break, I thought it might be useful to have some information about one another that we could explore further over the break."

"It is important for teams to get used to working together, so to begin with we're going to have an opportunity to practice a bit."

"I'm going to ask you to do something that you would probably never choose to do yourself. However, this particular task has relevance to what we'll be doing here today."

"Groups often work together better when they have information about one another. I have an activity that will allow us to get to know one another, and have fun in the process."

"Now we'll do an icebreaker. I know for some of you that signals pain and suffering, but, just think, by participating you will be adding to the joy of others who can't wait to do this."

"There's a reason for everything that happens. Now, the reason I just said that is because I'm going to introduce an activity that you may not see a purpose for immediately. Trust me, at the end I'll explain the relevance for us here today."

"We have been sitting for a long time. It is time for a stretch break."

"It's always helpful to know who your friends and enemies are. For this next activity, you had better hope the people in this room are your friends."

"I included the fact that I've written books on icebreakers as the last line on the bio. That was read so you would have fair warning about what I intended to do first."

Now you add your own openings....

Closing. . .

"Thank you for indulging me."

"Now that wasn't so bad, was it?"

"Now, that we have shared so many of our idiosyncrasies, we have nothing else to fear."

"You have proven that as a team you will make it—at least when doing icebreakers."

"I hope you've learned something about yourself and others that will be helpful. . ."

"What have you learned about each other?"

Now you add your own closings....

Edie's Top Ten Icebreakers

1. **All Aboard.** This is great for any kind of large-group training session.
2. **Beanbag Bungle.** They say throwing things is therapeutic.
3. **Double Take.** We pride ourselves in being different, but are we really?
4. **Great Shake.** You will recognize your most recent encounters!
5. **It's Who You Know.** Can you top this?
6. **Pick Pocket.** We carry our lives with us.
7. **Poetry in Motion.** A little rhythm and rhyme and we'll have a good time!
8. **Ride 'Em Cowboy.** Spend a night at the ol' corral.
9. **Repeat Performance.** Performance, performance, performance...
10. **Yellow Pages.** Let your fingers do the walking!

"Find the Perfect Icebreaker" Matrix

	Staff Meetings	Sales Meetings	Complete Strangers	Groups of 20 or More	Team Building	Pure Fun	Introducing a Topic	Outdoors	Self-Disclosure	Stuffy, Conservative	Waiting to Start	Everyday Living	Super Intelligent	Page Number
All Aboard			•	•		•		•						135
Arrivals and Departures	•						•			•		•		115
Baggage Claim			•			•					•			45
Beanbag Bungle		•		•		•		•				•		99
Biggest Deal		•	•			•						•		205
Birth Right		•		•					•					23
Born on the …			•	•							•	•		213
Briefcase Stickers		•			•		•				•		•	187
Canine Kibitzing			•	•		•								63
Constructive Feedback							•		•	•				119
Continuous Improvement	•	•								•				173
Crazy Captions		•			•									81
Domino Race						•	•				•			101
Double Take		•	•	•										25
First Real Job		•			•		•		•		•		•	85
Great Shake		•	•							•				31
Hand Jive		•		•		•								35
Happy Birthday!				•		•			•			•		153
Heart-to-Heart	•				•	•								3
High Note	•	•						•						5
If I Had a Hammer						•	•						•	121
In Basket	•		•				•				•			195
In Shape				•		•		•						137
It's Who You Know			•	•		•								49
Job Market		•	•	•		•						•		67
Key to My Heart					•	•			•					155
Line Up				•	•	•								87
Longest List		•			•	•							•	223

	Staff Meetings	Sales Meetings	Complete Strangers	Groups of 20 or More	Team Building	Pure Fun	Introducing a Topic	Outdoors	Self-Disclosure	Stuffy, Conservative	Waiting to Start	Everyday Living	Super Intelligent	Page Number
Mergers and Acquisitions		•											•	231
Most Like Me			•		•				•					159
Motor Mania			•		•	•		•		•				103
Nature Calls					•		•			•				125
New Team					•		•			•				91
News and Views				•						•	•		•	191
One Liners	•									•		•	•	227
Open Dialogue			•	•			•							51
Pass the Buck		•	•	•										71
Peculiarities		•	•			•					•			105
Phobia Mania			•			•				•			•	175
Pick Pocket			•		•	•	•			•	•			53
Piece by Piece	•				•					•				9
Poetry in Motion				•		•		•						109
Polyester Triathlon		•		•				•	•					141
Predictions		•			•	•	•		•				•	219
Repeat Performance		•		•			•							73
Return on Investment	•						•			•		•		211
Ride 'em, Cowboy				•		•		•						145
Road Signs		•					•			•				177
Simon Sez			•	•	•					•		•		75
Sounds of the Surf					•	•		•				•		209
Sports Fans			•	•	•	•								57
Star Light, Star Bright	•				•				•					13
Starting Over					•				•		•	•		199
Striking Resemblance					•			•	•					163
Superlatives					•	•			•					93

	Staff Meetings	Sales Meetings	Complete Strangers	Groups of 20 or More	Team Building	Pure Fun	Introducing a Topic	Outdoors	Self-Disclosure	Stuffy, Conservative	Waiting to Start	Everyday Living	Super Intelligent	Page Number
The Color of Love			•		•				•					167
The Numbers Game					•						•	•	•	203
The Waves			•	•						•		•		149
Tiddlywinks	•						•			•				181
Tools-for-the-Trade			•				•			•			•	229
Traffic Noises		•												39
Warning Signs					•		•						•	129
What Would You Do?	•				•				•		•			193
Yellow Pages	•				•		•				•			17
You Are What You Read	•								•	•				183

Icebreakers for
Staff Meetings

1. HEART-TO-HEART

PURPOSE

Staff Meetings; Team Building; Pure Fun

GROUP SIZE

6 to 20

LEVEL OF PHYSICAL ACTIVITY

Low

ESTIMATED TIME

3 to 8 minutes

PROPS

Small candy hearts with sayings on them (at least one per person), usually found in stores around February 14.

This activity provides a nonthreatening environment in which participants can say what's in their "hearts." Use it when a situation warrants focusing on one individual.

INSTRUCTIONS

1. Give each participant one candy heart.
2. Tell participants they'll now have a chance to give a wish to the person they're celebrating, such as when a person is leaving the company or is having a birthday.
3. Explain that each participant will think of a wish or statement about the person they're celebrating that incorporates the words found in their hearts.

4. Tell them they'll take turns expressing their wishes aloud to that person.

1. Have participants give hearts to many people.
2. Have participants choose the hearts they would like to use in forming their comments.

1. Keep this light and fun.
2. Don't be surprised if people use the opportunity to truly speak from their hearts.

2. HIGH NOTE

PURPOSE

Staff Meetings; Sales Meetings;
Introducing a Topic

GROUP SIZE

4 to 10

LEVEL OF PHYSICAL ACTIVITY

Low

ESTIMATED TIME

5 to 8 minutes

PROPS

Copies of the High Note Activity Sheet for all participants

This activity encourages quick situation analysis. Participants may find extremes difficult to define, but they will find the process helpful in creating a more objective arena for discussion.

INSTRUCTIONS

1. Give participants Notes Page.
2. Remind them that we often use the expressions "That ended on a high note" or "The meeting ended on a low note." Explain that it is often helpful to hear the high, medium, and low notes of an issue prior to holding a full discussion.

3. Ask them to take 2 minutes to record on their sheets their high, medium, and low notes on the topic the group is about to discuss.

4. After 2 minutes, ask them to "Tune in to the notes of others as you share with the people in your group what you've written on the paper."

5. Tell groups to designate a recorder who will capture the responses of the group.

VARIATIONS

1. Ask participants to work in pairs or groups to come up with the low, medium, and high notes.

2. At the end of the session, return to the high and low notes to see if they've been adequately addressed.

TIPS

1. This activity can be either serious or lighthearted.

2. Talk about the idea that the combination of notes creates harmony of thought.

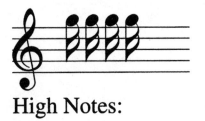

High Notes:

Medium Notes:

Low Notes:

3. PIECE BY PIECE

PURPOSE

Staff Meetings; Team Building; Pure Fun; Stuffy, Conservative Types

GROUP SIZE

8 to 40

LEVEL OF PHYSICAL ACTIVITY

High

ESTIMATED TIME

15 to 20 minutes

PROPS

One 50-piece puzzle and 4 small bags per group of four

Participants enjoy this activity because it engages them in cooperation quickly. Use it at any time to make a point about interdependence, the necessity of having everyone's input, or the importance of regular communication; or use it as an activity for competition or just for the fun of it.

INSTRUCTIONS

1. Divide the pieces from each puzzle into four small bags.
2. Put one complete puzzle—four bags—on each table.
3. Organize participants into groups of four.
4. Tell each participant to take a bag.

5. Explain that they are going to put a puzzle together with their tablemates, but they have to follow your instructions closely:

   - For the first 2 minutes, they should begin putting their puzzle pieces together by alternating turns. One person should put down a piece, then the next person should put down a piece, and so on. They should do this without talking or touching one another's pieces.

   - When the leader indicates that 2 minutes have passed, they should continue taking turns putting down pieces in silence, but they may begin touching one another's pieces. Continue for 2 minutes.

   - Finally, they will have 5 minutes to finish putting the puzzle together in any way they would like. Talking will be permitted during the last 5 minutes.

6. Begin the activity and monitor its timing by letting the group know when the first 2-minute period and the second 2-minute period are up.

7. After the final 5 minutes, stop the puzzle making.

8. Ask participants for observations and insights they gained from the activity.

VARIATIONS

1. Have groups put puzzles together without restrictions. Ask participants to explain how they cooperated or collaborated.

2. Give groups the same puzzles and make completion of the activity competitive.

TIPS

1. After asking for participant insights, include these points if they've been left out:

- We often do our own thing in isolation, without involving others whose pieces need to fit with ours.

- We often use only one mode of communication to get something done.

- When we involve one another, using all of the pieces and communicating in many different ways, we have a greater chance for successful completion of a project.

2. Choose puzzles that have messages or pictures that relate in some way to the content of the program or to the group.

4. STAR LIGHT, STAR BRIGHT

PURPOSE

> Staff Meetings; Team Building; Self-Disclosure

GROUP SIZE

> 6 to 18

LEVEL OF PHYSICAL ACTIVITY

> Medium

ESTIMATED TIME

> 6 to 8 minutes

PROPS

> Star Light, Star Bright Activity Sheets, one per participant
>
> This activity applies the age-old method of wishing upon a star to improve group communication and set goals. It makes a nice culminating activity for a team-building session. Use it anytime you want people to think about possibilities rather than impossibilities.

INSTRUCTIONS

> 1. Ask participants whether they have heard the poem, "Star light, star bright, first star I see tonight; I wish I may, I wish I might, have the wish I wish tonight." Explain that children are encouraged to say this and then make a wish when they see the glimmer of the first star in the sky.

2. Encourage participants to think of a wish that they have for the team, if their time together has shown them a glimmer of hope.

3. Pass out the stars and ask participants to write their wishes for the team on the stars.

4. When they've finished, ask participants to stand in a circle. Explain that their sky is now the floor in front of them.

5. Repeat the rhyme. When you finish, ask participants come forward one at a time to place their stars in the circle on the floor and state their wishes.

VARIATION

Have participants place stars in a cluster on the wall.

TIPS

1. This activity may be light or serious. Respect the tone.

2. You can buy sky charts upon which participants could place the stars.

5. YELLOW PAGES

PURPOSE

Staff Meetings; Team Building; Introducing a Topic

GROUP SIZE

4 to 40

LEVEL OF PHYSICAL ACTIVITY

Low

ESTIMATED TIME

5 to 10 minutes

PROPS

One copy of Yellow Pages Activity Sheet and one copy of telephone or World Wide Web Yellow Pages per group (or a listing of categories from the Yellow Pages)

This is a humorous activity that stimulates healthy interaction and gives people a chance to vent. Use it as a brainstorming activity, as a team evaluation activity, or for pure fun.

INSTRUCTIONS

1. Organize participants into groups of 2 to 6.
2. Give each group a Yellow Pages Activity Sheet and a copy of telephone or World Wide Web Yellow Pages.
3. Explain that often unexpected categories in the Yellow Pages will address topics. For example, if the topic were fisheries or evaluation program, a helpful Yellow Pages category might be "Scales."

4. Ask each group to name topics of interest to them, or goals they have for the organization.

5. Tell groups they have 5 minutes to decide on the Yellow Pages categories for each topic.

6. After 5 minutes, ask groups to report their responses.

VARIATIONS

1. Make this a creativity contest. Ask groups to name their own categories and put the work of the organization into categories.

2. Ask individuals rather than groups to complete the Activity Sheets.

TIPS

1. This should be a fun activity. Keep it light.

2. Allow more time if participants are really getting into the activity.

Choose two Yellow Pages category for each topic listed below. Explain why you selected that topic. Be prepared to share your choices.

Topic 1: <u>Teambuilding</u> _____

Topic 2: <u>Leadership</u> _____

Topic 3: <u>Ethics</u> _____

Topic 4: <u>Informational Technology</u> _____

Topic 5: <u>Quality</u> _____

Topic 6: <u>Hiring and Recruiting</u> _____

Topic 7: <u>Improvising</u> _____

Topic 8: <u>Strategic Planning</u> _____

Or create your own:

Topic 1:

Topic 2:

Topic 3:

Icebreakers for Sales Meetings

6. BIRTH RIGHT

PURPOSE

Sales Meetings; Groups of 20 or More; Self-Disclosure

GROUP SIZE

15 to 50

LEVEL OF PHYSICAL ACTIVITY

High

ESTIMATED TIME

5 to 7 minutes

PROPS

None

Grouping participants by birth order is a fun way for people to relate to one another, whether they already know each other or not. Use Birth Right at the beginning of a session as a mixer or after lunch as an energizer.

INSTRUCTIONS

1. Explain to participants that:
    a. Birth order plays a role in our childhood development.
    b. Common experiences and feelings are often shared by people of the same birth order.
    c. This is an opportunity for them to discover those commonalties.

2. Ask participants to group themselves into four corners of the room by the following birth orders: oldest, youngest, middle, and only child. Explain that *middle* means anyone who is not an oldest, youngest, or only child.

3. After participants are grouped, tell them they have 2 minutes to answer and record their agreed-upon responses to the following questions:

   a. What were the advantages of being a(n) _____ child?

   b. What were the disadvantages of being a(n) _____ child?

4. After 2 minutes, ask each group to read its list.

VARIATIONS

1. Before step 2, have people list the advantages of being a(n) _____ child on one side of a 3 × 5-inch card and on the other side, list the disadvantages of that position. Then when they move to Step 3, encourage them to share cards and come to agreement on a few in each category.

2. Ask each group to simply demonstrate one advantage and one disadvantage, which the other groups will guess.

3. Ask participants to think of their order in the organization: new hire; employed for one to two years; employed for a while; employed forever (or at least it seems that way).

TIPS

1. Have fun playing with this activity. You'll find that participants will refer back to it often during the session.

2. If you know nothing about birth order, get a book from the library or purchase a book to help you understand the power of this activity.

7. DOUBLE TAKE

PURPOSE

Sales Meetings; Complete Strangers; Groups of 20 or More

GROUP SIZE

20 to 500

LEVEL OF PHYSICAL ACTIVITY

High

ESTIMATED TIME

3 to 5 minutes

PROPS

Upbeat music on tape or disk; Double Take Activity Sheet for leader

In this activity, participants pair up by finding common ground, whether it be a similar hair color or a passion for pizza. Double Take is a fun, simple way for people to mingle in a non-threatening way. Use it with an active group of people, whether they know one another or not.

I don't know where the phrase "double take" came from, but I have my suspicions. Perhaps "double take" was coined by a teenager coming into the house after school, finding Mom in the middle of mixing chocolate chip cookie dough, taking a taste on the tip of a finger, ignoring Mom's cries of alarm, and then taking another.

1. Ask participants to stand and move to a location in the room where they can walk around and mingle freely.

2. Tell participants that when the music begins, they should begin shaking hands with people and introducing or re-introducing themselves.

3. Explain to them that they will have an opportunity to "do a double take" with another participant.

4. Tell them that you will call out a characteristic that they may have in common with another group member. They should immediately find another person who shares that particular characteristic. For instance, if you call out "hair color," they should form a pair with a person who has the same hair color.

5. Explain that you will call out many characterisitics and each time they should "do a double take" with a new person.

6. Begin the activity, using the activity sheet provided.

VARIATIONS

1. If the group is small, ask participants to think of a way they could form a pair with another person and engage that person. Give them five chances to do this with five differ-ent people.

2. Use this activity to create groups of four to six people and change the name of the activity to Group Take.

TIPS

1. Blow a whistle each time you call out a different word or phrase.

2. Use some words or phrases that are particular to the group.

3. For each item, there may be people who have not found a "double take." You might acknowledge that by asking for a

show of hands in response to the question: "Who has not found a double take?" Moving on quickly to the next item will allow those individuals to make a "double take."

DOUBLE TAKE ACTIVITY SHEET (FOR THE LEADER)

Hair color

Eye color

Shoe size

Favorite color

Age

Pet ownership

Same color shirt

Favorite pizza topping

Height

Favorite food

Music preference

Favorite sport

Favorite team

Type of car

Length of daily commute

8. GREAT SHAKE

PURPOSE

Sales Meetings; Complete Strangers; Stuffy, Conservative Types

GROUP SIZE

20 to 250

LEVEL OF PHYSICAL ACTIVITY

High

ESTIMATED TIME

2 to 4 minutes

PROPS

Great Shake Activity Sheet for leader

This icebreaker gets people moving around, shaking hands, and introducing themselves to one another. Use it with people who don't know one another at all or very well, both as a way to meet and as a way to group themselves for further small group activities.

INSTRUCTIONS

1. Ask participants to pair up with someone they don't know to practice types of handshakes.
2. Describe three types of handshakes from the descriptions on the Great Shake Activity Sheet: the Vise, the Pump, the Sway, the Topper, or the Flip. As you describe each one, encourage participants to practice with their partners.

3. Tell them they'll have a chance to get in sync with their partners.

4. Explain that you'll count to three and say "Great shake." When you say "Great shake," they're to use one of the learned handshakes with their partners.

5. After they've done it once, ask how many partners used the same shake.

6. Do it two more times.

VARIATIONS

1. Encourage them to walk around shaking hands and to use a variety of the handshakes.

2. Ask people to use their favorite handshake.

3. Have partners try any handshakes and then share which kinds of handshakes they usually use.

TIP

Have fun with modeling the handshakes as you explain each one. Dramatize as much as you dare.

The Vise—Grab that other hand and grip like you mean it. The goal is intimidation.

The Pump—Pump, pump, pump it up. You'll actually get your heart rate up as you shake hands while pumping your partner's hand up and down.

The Sway—When you take your partner's hand in yours, start swaying it back and forth between you, from left to right, as if you're holding hands or jumping rope.

The Topper—This type of handshaker puts the second hand on top of yours to make a hand sandwich, thinking this added touch lets you know that he or she really means it. Does it?

The Flip—Even a handshake can be a power trip with this one. When you take your partner's hand, flip it over so yours is on top.

9. HAND JIVE

PURPOSE

Sales Meetings; Groups of 20 or More; Pure Fun

GROUP SIZE

20 to 60

LEVEL OF PHYSICAL ACTIVITY

Medium

ESTIMATED TIME

8 to 10 minutes

PROPS

Copies of pictures of hands in four to six different positions (one position for each group you want to form)

An activity like this stays with participants throughout the session. After the icebreaker, you will find these hand gestures being used in a playful manner.

INSTRUCTIONS

1. Give each participant one hand picture.
2. Explain to the group that their job is to find the other people in their group by looking for those who are holding their hands in the same position.
3. When groups have formed, tell them they have 5 minutes to create a sales slogan that relates somehow to their group's hand position. (E.g., pinch— "_____ is so wonderful, I have to pinch myself to believe it's true.")

4. After 5 minutes, ask each group to show its hand position and repeat its slogan.

VARIATIONS

1. Put participants in groups and have them decide on a hand position or movement that signifies their group.

2. Ask groups to create a slogan using many different hand positions.

TIP

You can play on the groups' "handiness" for the rest of the session.

HAND JIVE ACTIVITY SHEET

Grasping

Open

Pinching

Pointing

Thumbs Up

Victory

10. TRAFFIC NOISE

PURPOSE

Sales Meetings

GROUP SIZE

18 to 40

LEVEL OF PHYSICAL ACTIVITY

Medium

ESTIMATED TIME

2 to 5 minutes

PROPS

Traffic Noise Activity Sheet, one card per person and one vehicle per group you wish to form

I have found this activity to be a high-energy, fun way to get people into groups at any point during a session when participants are open to a playful moment.

INSTRUCTIONS

1. Explain that you are introducing an activity that will organize participants into groups, an activity called Traffic Noise. Tell them that they will be creating traffic noise in the room.
2. Give each participant a picture of a type of vehicle. (The number of different vehicles you use should match the number of groups you wish to form.)

3. Invite participants to group themselves by their vehicle's sound. In other words, they should "drive through" the group, imitating the sound their vehicle makes.

4. Explain that when they find other participants who have the same vehicle (because hopefully they'll be making a similar sound), they should join together, continue "driving around," and listen for other vehicles who are speaking the same language.

5. When all participants are in their vehicle groups, ask each group to make its vehicle sound collectively for the other groups to hear.

VARIATIONS

1. If participants in the vehicle group don't know each other well, invite them to introduce themselves, saying where they are from, what they do, etc. If they already know each other well, ask them to talk about the topic of the session or their reasons for participating in the session.

2. While the groups are making their collective sounds, encourage them to truly get into gear and move like their vehicles move.

TIPS

1. Use this activity with a group of participants who don't mind acting out.

2. This activity works best with participants who don't know each other well.

TRAFFIC NOISE ACTIVITY SHEET

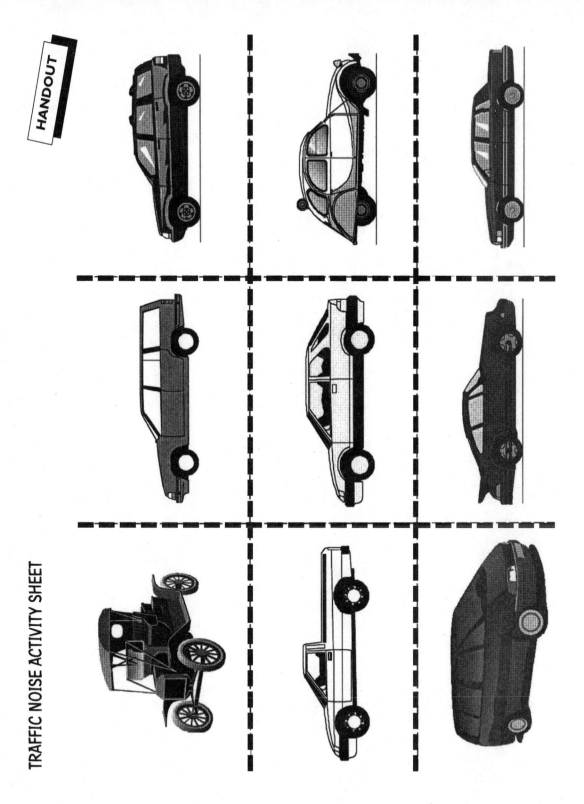

41

Icebreakers for Complete Strangers

11. BAGGAGE CLAIM

PURPOSE

Complete Strangers; Pure Fun

GROUP SIZE

12 to 500

LEVEL OF PHYSICAL ACTIVITY

Medium

ESTIMATED TIME

15 to 20 minutes

PROPS

Baggage cards, one per participant

In this activity, people find things out about each other before putting faces to names. It's best used with people who don't know one another well, because they will be moving around and meeting each other.

INSTRUCTIONS

1. Pass out cards to participants and ask them to "pack their bags" by filling in the blanks.
2. Explain that they will now experience going to the baggage claim area and accidentally picking up someone else's bag.
3. Ask participants to walk around the room, shaking hands and introducing themselves to other participants in the following way:

- The first time a person shakes hands with another person, both participants will introduce themselves and tell each other what is in their bags (based on the information they wrote on the card).

- The pair will then exchange "bags" and move on to greet other participants.

- As they greet other participants, they will shake hands and introduce themselves but explain that they have the wrong "bags." They will then proceed to tell each other who their "bags" belong to and what's in them, using the information on the cards they have in their hands.

- After each meeting, they will "trade bags" and then move on to another participant.

4. After 5 minutes, ask participants to stop.

5. If the group has 40 or fewer participants, you can ask each person to read the name of the person whose card they are holding, introduce that person by what's in the bag, and return the card to that person, so that eventually everyone will be holding their own "baggage" again.

VARIATIONS

1. Ask the participants to draw their own luggage on cards.

2. If it is a small group, have participants "guess who" as each card is read.

TIPS

1. If you collect the cards, you can use them for drawings and door prizes.

2. Decorate the room with maps or travel posters.

BAGGAGE CLAIM ACTIVITY SHEET

Please "fill the bag" with five interesting
facts about your life.

Please "fill the bag" with five interesting
facts about your life.

Please "fill the bag" with five interesting
facts about your life.

Please "fill the bag" with five interesting
facts about your life.

Please "fill the bag" with five interesting
facts about your life.

Please "fill the bag" with five interesting
facts about your life.

12. IT'S *WHO* YOU KNOW

PURPOSE

> Complete Strangers; Groups of 20 or More; Pure Fun

GROUP SIZE

> 8 to 500

LEVEL OF PHYSICAL ACTIVITY

> Low

ESTIMATED TIME

> 5 to 7 minutes

PROPS

> None

People love to talk about the famous person they once met in an elevator, or ran into at the Burger King, or got an autograph from.

INSTRUCTIONS

1. Tell a story about a famous person you bumped into.
2. Ask for a show of hands of the people who have had the experience of being in the presence of a famous person—other than family members.
3. Explain that everyone loves to tell the story that starts, "You know who I ran into today?"
4. Tell participants to form groups of four.

5. Explain that they have 8 minutes to take turns telling their stories in the following manner:

   a. One person called Teller begins and describes a scenario in which he or she ran into a famous person, without telling who the famous person was.

   b. Other group members then guess who was the famous person.

   c. The person who guesses gets to be the Teller next. (If that person has already been the Teller, someone else goes next.)

6. After 4 minutes, remind the groups they only have 4 minutes left.

7. After 8 minutes, ask the entire group for a show of hands in response to the following questions:

   a. How many people named political figures?

   b. How many people named movie stars?

   c. How many people named religious figures?

   d. How many people named sports figures?

VARIATIONS

1. Use partners instead of groups of four, and limit the time to 5 minutes.

2. Ask participants only how many named movie stars, or other group members.

TIP

If there are relatively famous people (such as the boss) in the audience, this is a good time to introduce them.

13. OPEN DIALOGUE

PURPOSE

Complete Strangers; Groups of 20 or More; Introducing a Topic

GROUP SIZE

8 to 500

LEVEL OF PHYSICAL ACTIVITY

Low

ESTIMATED TIME

5 minutes

PROPS

None

Everyday keys open dialogue and allow for self-disclosure in a nonthreatening way. Use this activity with large groups of adults or small, for personal introductions or as a humor break.

INSTRUCTIONS

1. Ask participants to stand and find a partner.
2. Explain that we all carry keys with us that let us do things or get in places we need to enter.
3. Tell participants to take out the keys they have with them, in pockets or purses.

4. When participants have keys in hand, tell them they have one minute each to explain the purpose of each key to their partners.

5. After 2 minutes, ask those individuals who had a key with a defunct purpose to raise their hands.

VARIATIONS

1. Ask participants to guess the purpose of each other's keys.
2. Make this a small group activity.

TIP

Have fun with this activity; start off by explaining the purpose of each of the keys on your own ring.

14. PICK POCKET

PURPOSE

Complete Strangers; Team Building; Pure Fun; Introducing a Topic; Stuffy, Conservative Types

GROUP SIZE

8 to 24

LEVEL OF PHYSICAL ACTIVITY

Medium

ESTIMATED TIME

3 to 5 minutes

PROPS

Pick Pocket Activity Sheets, one per participant

This activity is an adult version of a scavenger hunt; participants get to "scavenge" through their pockets, wallets, purses, and briefcases to find the items on their lists. Use this at the beginning of a session for people to get to know one another, or midway through as an energizer.

INSTRUCTIONS

1. Organize participants into groups of five to ten.
2. Give each participant a Pick Pocket Activity Sheet.
3. Tell groups they have 2 minutes to come up with as many items from the list as they can. Tell them that each item is worth two points.

4. Explain that they may make a reasonable substitution, but if they do, that item will be worth only one point. For example, someone may have an Avis Preferred Renter card rather than a Hertz #1 Club Gold Card.

5. After 2 minutes, ask groups to count their points.

6. Ask groups to share what items they got from the list and which substitutions they made.

VARIATION

Give groups a blank sheet of paper and ask them to list things they had in their pockets or purses that they thought other groups might not have.

TIP

Give prizes to the group that has the most points.

Pick Pocket List

___ Picture of a close relative

___ Credit card without a signature

___ AAA card

___ Dry cleaner receipt

___ Grocery list

___ Original Social Security card

___ Voter registration card for a registered Democrat

___ Hertz #1 Club Gold Card

___ Buffalo nickel, wheat penny, or steel dime

___ Black comb

___ Electronic pager (beeper)

___ Swiss army knife

___ Money clip

___ Fitness club card

___ Sam's Club card with photo

___ Coupon for any food or restaurant item

___ A mint

___ Contact lens case

___ Matches from a restaurant in another state

___ Cloth handkerchief

15. SPORTS FANS

PURPOSE

Complete Strangers; Groups of 20 or More; Team Building; Pure Fun

GROUP SIZE

20 to 200

LEVEL OF PHYSICAL ACTIVITY

High

ESTIMATED TIME

3 to 5 minutes

PROPS

Sports Fans cards, one per participant

In this activity, people form groups by finding others who have the same sport card they do. To form groups at any time during a session, use this activity with groups that are willing to "play."

INSTRUCTIONS

1. Give each participant a Sports Fans card.
2. Organize participants in an open area of the room where they can move about.
3. Tell participants that they will be engaged in an activity called Sports Fans. Explain that there is no room for couch potatoes in this activity.

4. Explain that each person has a Sports Fans card with a picture representing a particular sport on the front. They are to find other participants who have the same sport and form a "team."

5. Tell them that the only catch is that they may not show the cards or speak any words; they must demonstrate the sport as they move about the room.

6. Explain that when they have found another person or persons who have the same sport, they should huddle together and continue the search for the rest of their team.

7. After 3 minutes, ask each group to quickly demonstrate its sport for other groups to see and guess.

VARIATION

Use particular kinds of sports only, such as summer sports, Olympic sports, etc.

TIP

Demonstrate yourself or ask a participant to demonstrate a sport for everyone to see before the activity begins.

SPORTS FANS ACTIVITY SHEET

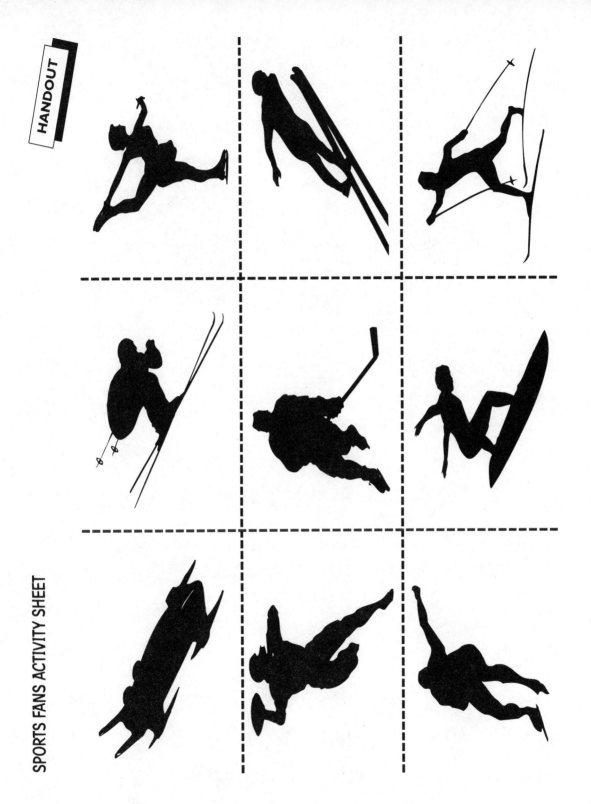

Icebreakers for Groups of 20 or More

16. CANINE KIBITZING

PURPOSE

Complete Strangers; Groups of 20 or More; Pure Fun

GROUP SIZE

24 to 60

LEVEL OF PHYSICAL ACTIVITY

High

ESTIMATED TIME

3 to 5 minutes

PROPS

Canine Kibitzing Activity Sheets, one card per participant

In this activity, participants are assigned a sound to make, and then asked to use this sound to bark their way into groups as they seek out other people making the same sound. Use this activity at any point in a session when you want to group and physically energize participants.

INSTRUCTIONS

1. Give each participant a card with a dog sound on it.
2. Tell them that in this activity they will be forming smaller groups. To do that you would like to introduce the languages of the canine community. Explain that many languages are represented in the group.

3. Instruct participants to begin their canine kibitzing by making the sounds on their cards. When they hear a bark, yap, or woof similar to their own, they should form a group with those canines and wait for others to do likewise.

4. When groups are formed, ask each to give its sound for the rest of the group to hear.

VARIATION

Any group of sounds will work for this familiar activity.

TIPS

1. The spin on this activity is the idea of different canine sounds. Play on that in your introduction.

2. Choose your group and activity carefully. I only use this activity with groups who are playful or less into their own self-importance.

3. Never refer to the participants as "dogs."

4. For a small group, use four sounds instead of six.

CANINE KIBITZING ACTIVITY SHEET

Growl

Ruff

Woof

Arf

Bark

Yap

17. JOB MARKET

PURPOSE

Sales Meetings; Complete Strangers; Groups of 20 or More; Pure Fun

GROUP SIZE

50 to 400

LEVEL OF PHYSICAL ACTIVITY

High

ESTIMATED TIME

7 to 10 minutes

PROPS

Open space; Job Market Activity Sheet for leader

In this activity, participants get to know others who are working in similar industries, and get to celebrate and commiserate with them.

INSTRUCTIONS

1. Explain to group that they will now have an opportunity to meet other people in their industries.
2. Ask the group to listen carefully for their industry and phrase as you read from the Job Market Activity Sheet.
3. Read the list of industries and phrases. Remind participants to remember their industry phrases.
4. Tell groups that when you say "Job market," that will signal the start of 3 minutes they have to find all the other

people in the room who are working in the same industry they are. The way they'll do this is to yell out their industry phrases, and join with others who are yelling the same phrase. Tell them to stay together once they've found one another.

5. After you've said "Job market" and allowed 3 minutes, tell them they have 4 minutes to agree on a word or phrase that most adequately describes the most positive thing about working in that industry, and a word or phrase that is descriptive of the most negative thing about working in that industry.

6. After 4 minutes, explain that you will name each industry, after which each group should shout the negative thing.

7. After the negative things, read the list of industries again and have them yell out the positive thing.

VARIATIONS

1. If you know who will be in attendance, assign them numbers or plan another way to assign them to industry groups when you are ready to do this activity. When they get into those groups, ask them to act out their industries for other groups to guess which industry they're representing.

2. If appropriate, use jobs rather than industries.

TIPS

1. This activity should generate spirit and enthusiasm. It is a great opening activity when people do not know one another.

2. It's okay if a certain amount of competition between groups develops.

List of Industries with Descriptive Phrases

1. Hospitality—We aim to please!

2. Manufacturing—We make it!

3. Retail and Wholesale—Sell! Sell! Sell!

4. Information Technology—We got mail!

5. Mining—Undercover agents!

6. Utilities—Power to the people!

7. Education—We know everything!

8. Tourism—Let us take you there!

9. Health care—Take a breath and hold it.

10. Construction—What a build!

11. Entertainment—Come and get it!

12. Archeology—We dig it!

13. Government—We rule!

14. Publishing and Printing—Mum's the Word!

15. Other—

18. PASS THE BUCK

PURPOSE

Sales Meetings; Complete Strangers; Groups of 20 or More

GROUP SIZE

20 to 500

LEVEL OF PHYSICAL ACTIVITY

Low

ESTIMATED TIME

5 to 8 minutes

PROPS

None

People love "buying" valuable information and finding out about their neighbors at the same time.

INSTRUCTIONS

1. Ask participants to take a $1 bill out of their pockets or purses and hold it in the air.
2. Tell those who don't have a $1 bill to hold a $5 bill or other denomination (such as a quarter) in the air.
3. Ask them to find someone near them who is holding up the same denomination, and partner with that person.
4. Explain that they will have an opportunity now to share valuable pieces of information that they often don't get to share, and get paid for that information.

5. Tell them the catch is that their partners have to decide whether the information has value.

6. Give participants these instructions:

   a. Share a piece of information with your partner that you think he or she will want to know.

   b. If your partner thinks that information is of value, the partner will give you the bill in hand. If the partner doesn't deem the information to be of value (perhaps because it's already known, or because it's not relevant to the partner's experiences), the partner will ask for more information, and you need to oblige.

   c. Once your partner has heard enough information of value, he or she will "pay" you for it.

   d. It then becomes the other partner's turn.

VARIATIONS

1. Form small groups. As each person shares his or her information, the first person to speak up about the value of the information gets to "pay" for it. Once people have used their buck, though, they may not "pay" for any other information.

2. Have individuals negotiate the value before settling on the amount.

TIPS

1. Play up the idea of the value of information in your introduction. Use examples like knowing who a person is or having a stock market tip.

2. If participants don't have any money with them, tell them they can use things such as pencils or business cards. The catch is that their partners must use the same items.

19. REPEAT PERFORMANCE

PURPOSE

Sales Meetings; Groups of 20 or More; Introducing a Topic

GROUP SIZE

60 to 500

LEVEL OF PHYSICAL ACTIVITY

Medium

ESTIMATED TIME

3 to 5 minutes

PROPS

None

In this activity, your audience enjoys taking part in the speech you are delivering. Use this activity to maintain interest and add humor to your speech.

INSTRUCTIONS

1. Decide on two specific words or phrases that you would like participants to walk away from your speech remembering.
2. After you are introduced, explain to the audience that you would like them to participate in your speech.
3. Explain that they will have an opportunity for involvement throughout the speech by shouting out certain words when you point to them with your right hand, and certain

other words when you point with your left hand. (For instance, if you choose the words "yes" and "no," you would ask questions periodically during the speech and point at the audience for the response. Example: "Would you like to see this company become more successful because of your efforts in selling?")

4. Ask participants to practice with you one time. Point with your right hand and then with your left.

VARIATIONS

1. Ask other people to indicate when the audience should respond (such as others on the platform with you).

2. Tell a story that could have a repeated line, and ask participants to repeat the line any time you point to them.

TIPS

1. If people don't get into this immediately, make them practice again until they "get it right."

2. Have fun yourself, and the audience will too.

20. SIMON SEZ

PURPOSE

Complete Strangers; Groups of 20 or More; Team Building

GROUP SIZE

10 to 200

LEVEL OF PHYSICAL ACTIVITY

Medium to high

ESTIMATED TIME

5 minutes

PROPS

Simon Sez Activity Sheet for leader

This is a well-known activity that gets attention, creates energy and laughter, and gains the participation of everyone. Use it in a speech to a large audience, or as a break during a long meeting.

INSTRUCTIONS

1. Ask participants to stand and get ready to play Simon Sez.
2. Explain the simple rules: When you say "Simon sez" followed by an order, the group should obey the order; when you give an order without saying "Simon sez," they should not follow the order.

3. Give the orders. After each order, tell people who were correct in following the orders to remain standing, and ask people who were wrong to sit down.

4. When finished, announce that the people still standing are the winners.

VARIATION

Ask a participant to lead the Simon Sez session.

TIPS

1. Keep things moving quickly. If you delay, no one will make a mistake.

2. If everyone does what they're supposed to, make a remark about the astuteness of the group and move on.

SIMON SEZ ACTIVITY SHEET

1. Simon sez lift your right hand into the air.
2. Simon sez lift your left hand into the air.
3. Put your right hand down.
4. Simon sez put your left hand down.
5. Simon sez point upward with your right hand.
6. Simon sez point downward with your left hand.
7. Simon sez point both hands toward yourself.
8. Point both hands toward your neighbors.
9. Simon sez stop pointing and sit down.
10. Simon sez stand up.
11. Simon sez stand on one leg.
12. Stand on both legs.
13. Simon sez shake hands with one neighbor.
14. Simon sez shake hands with another neighbor.
15. Simon sez turn around.
16. Turn back and face front.
17. Simon sez turn back and face front.
18. Give yourselves a hand.
19. Simon sez give yourselves a hand.

Icebreakers for Team Building

---

21. CRAZY CAPTIONS

PURPOSE

Sales Meetings; Team Building

GROUP SIZE

8 to 24

LEVEL OF PHYSICAL ACTIVITY

Medium

ESTIMATED TIME

2 to 4 minutes

PROPS

Crazy Captions Activity Sheets, one per participant

Participants work together to create captions for a series of given pictures. Use this activity to encourage people to work together in pairs at any point in the session that calls for an energizer.

INSTRUCTIONS

1. Organize participants into pairs.
2. Give each participant a Crazy Captions Activity Sheet.
3. Tell pairs they have one minute to write a caption under each picture.
4. After one minute or so, ask pairs to share their captions.

VARIATIONS

1. Make it an individual activity; pass out activity sheets as people are entering the session and share their captions later.

2. Have groups come up with captions.

3. Choose your own pictures for captions.

TIP

This activity is purely for fun.

CRAZY CAPTIONS ACTIVITY SHEET

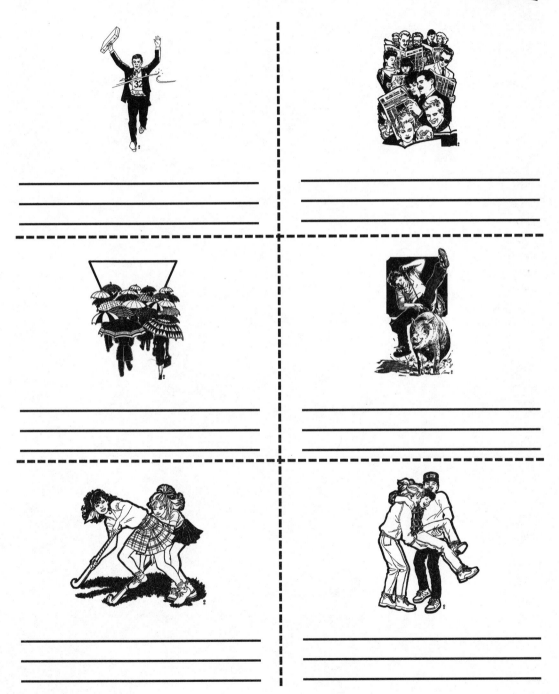

22. FIRST REAL JOB

PURPOSE

Complete Strangers; Team Building; Introducing a Topic; Self-Disclosure

GROUP SIZE

10 to 500

LEVEL OF PHYSICAL ACTIVITY

Low

ESTIMATED TIME

5 to 7 minutes

PROPS

None

People get an entrée into the job market in a variety of ways, all of which serve as "schools of practicality." In this activity people share first job experiences and the understanding they gleaned from those experiences.

INSTRUCTIONS

1. Organize participants into pairs.
2. Explain that all of us have a story or two to share about our "first real job" experiences. All of us can point to some thing or things we learned from that first job.
3. Tell pairs they have 5 minutes to share with one another their "first real job" experiences and then reveal what they learned from their time on those jobs.

4. After 5 minutes, follow one of two next steps:

   a. If the group is large, explain that most people begin their job experience with a "first real job" in the retail or hospitality industries. Ask for a show of hands first jobs were in each of those industries and then do the same for other industries.

   b. If the group is small, quickly hear from each pair.

5. To insert humor, ask for a show of hands of how many people learned that they didn't want to keep doing that job.

VARIATIONS

1. Organize participants into groups of four or five. Ask them to find something in common about their "first real job" experiences.

2. Make this a more serious activity by asking participants to share experiences about their "first real job" in their careers, rather than describing any "first real job."

TIP

Have fun with this by telling a story about a person you recently encountered who you could tell was in a first real job, or by telling a story about your own first real job.

23. LINE UP

PURPOSE

Groups of 20 or More; Team Building; Pure Fun

GROUP SIZE

16 to 200

LEVEL OF PHYSICAL ACTIVITY

High

ESTIMATED TIME

5 to 7 minutes

PROPS

Line Up Activity Sheet for leader

Lining up by height order or alphabetically is just the beginning in this activity, as participants think of creative ways to line up in order. Use this activity to break the monotony of long periods of sitting, and you'll find participants finding out about each other too. Any group is game for this activity.

INSTRUCTIONS

1. Organize participants into groups of 8 to 20.
2. Tell participants that in the Line Up, they will have a chance to learn things about one another they may never think to ask.
3. Give these instructions:
   - This is group competition.

- I will give the instruction for groups to line up in a particular way.

- Your group should get in line as quickly as possible.

- When your group is lined up appropriately, but not before, all group members should clap to indicate your readiness to me.

4. Conduct a practice round. Tell them to line up by height, and to clap when they're finished.

5. Begin the activity. After each lineup, determine which group clapped first and then announce them as the winner of that round.

VARIATIONS

1. Use this activity periodically throughout a long session.

2. Ask groups to come up with their own way of letting you know they're ready. (I've had groups yell something, hum a song, put up their hands, etc.) This adds a lot to the fun.

TIPS

1. Keep the tone light; this is a fun competition.

2. Laugh and play with humorous comments from participants; there will be many.

3. Remember political correctness with regard to your own or participants' comments.

1. Line up in order by shoe size.

2. Line up in order by length of arm's reach.

3. Line up in order alphabetically by favorite color.

4. Line up in order by number of siblings you have.

5. Line up in order by hair color, lightest to darkest.

6. Line up in order by age, youngest to oldest.

7. Line up in order by length of time with current employer.

8. Line up in order alphabetically by first name.

9. Line up in order alphabetically by last name.

10. Line up in order by number of pets owned.

11. Line up in order by hair length, longest to shortest.

12. Line up in order by the number of bones you've ever broken.

24. NEW TEAM

PURPOSE

Team Building; Pure Fun; Stuffy, Conservative Types

GROUP SIZE

10 to 60

LEVEL OF PHYSICAL ACTIVITY

Low

ESTIMATED TIME

5 to 10 minutes

PROPS

None

A truism about building teams is that the dynamic in a team changes when members either leave or enter the team. This activity helps participants realize the significance of that statement. This activity is best used during a session about teams.

INSTRUCTIONS

1. Organize participants into teams of five to eight.
2. Use one self-disclosure activity and one team-building activity with the teams to get them used to interacting with one another.
3. After a morning or day of team building, arbitrarily select one team member from each team and move them into a different team.
4. Lead the teams through a different team activity.

5. When that activity is completed, ask each team to explain the differences in team dynamics with their newly created team.

6. Ask the group to explain the significance of this observation.

VARIATION

Change two or three team members rather than only one.

TIPS

1. There is significant learning in this exercise.

2. Keep the discussion focused on the dynamics of membership changes, rather than on members themselves.

25. SUPERLATIVES

PURPOSE

Team Building; Pure Fun; Self-Disclosure

GROUP SIZE

6 to 60

LEVEL OF PHYSICAL ACTIVITY

Medium

ESTIMATED TIME

5 to 10 minutes

PROPS

Superlatives Activity Sheets, one per participant

In this activity, participants write down things about themselves and share them with others. This is a good activity for team building or for people to get to know one another better. Use it in the beginning of a session, or before a section that deals with roles or understanding interdependence.

INSTRUCTIONS

1. Organize participants into groups of five to six.
2. Explain that many U.S. high schools in the 1960s, 1970s, and 1980s had a "Superlatives" selection in senior year. Those superlatives often included Most Intellectual, Best Looking, Class Clown, and Most Likely to Succeed. The difficulty with that method is the comparing that takes place between students to come up with one winner. Taking a developmental approach means looking at oneself and asking,

"When am I most likely to succeed?" or "How am I most talented?"

3. Pass out Superlatives Activity Sheets to participants and ask them to take one minute to complete them.

4. After one minute, ask participants to partner up and take another minute to share their sheets (each person having 30 seconds).

5. After one minute, ask them to introduce their partners to the rest of their small groups, including the information on the sheets.

VARIATION

Rather than using the categories on the activity sheet, ask participants to come up with their own superlatives about themselves.

TIPS

1. You might want to play some music from the 1960s, 1970s, or 1980s before or during this activity.

2. This activity is meant to be kept light. Encourage participant humor through examples of your own.

3. Fill out a sheet for yourself and use some of your answers for examples. You might say, "I am best dressed when I am in my old blue comfortable sweats and my new Nike sneakers."

SUPERLATIVES ACTIVITY SHEET

Fill in the space after each statement.

1. I am "most talented" when I am:

2. I am "most likely to succeed" when I am:

3. I am "most versatile" when I am:

4. I am "best looking" when I am:

5. I am "class clown" when I am:

6. I am "best dressed" when I am:

7. I am the "best dancer" when I am:

8. I am "most friendly" when I am:

9. I like myself best when I am:

Icebreakers for Pure Fun

26. BEANBAG BUNGLE

PURPOSE

Sales Meetings; Groups of 20 or More; Pure Fun; Outdoors

GROUP SIZE

12 to 84

LEVEL OF PHYSICAL ACTIVITY

High

ESTIMATED TIME

3 to 6 minutes

PROPS

Three beanbags for each group of 12

Participants toss a beanbag around the group until each person has a chance to catch and throw. The trick is, they have to toss it in the same order each time. Use this as a challenge with any group that would welcome an energizer.

INSTRUCTIONS

1. Ask participants to stand and move apart so there's space between them.
2. Explain the rules:
   - The object of the activity is for the group to establish a forward and reverse pattern while throwing one beanbag around, then repeat the same pattern with two more beanbags added.

- The first person will pass the beanbag; wait until the fifth person in the pattern has caught it and pass another beanbag; wait until the fifth person in the pattern has caught it and pass the third beanbag.
- The last person who gets the first beanbag reverses the pattern by throwing it back to the person who threw it to him or her, and he does the same with the other two beanbags.
- Play continues until all beanbags are back in the possession of the first person who started the pattern.

3. Begin a practice round with only one beanbag.

VARIATION

Use a Koosh® ball, beach ball or other object.

TIPS

1. If the group is good at the game, add a fourth beanbag.
2. Some groups can only be successful with one beanbag. If they're having difficulty during the practice round, use only one beanbag.
3. Naturally, some people will bungle the beanbags. Encourage them to pick them up and keep them moving. If they can't, begin again.
4. Part of the fun is the bungling of beanbags as they pass, going forward and in reverse at the same time.

27. DOMINO RACE

PURPOSE

Pure Fun; Introducing a Topic; Stuffy, Conservative Types

GROUP SIZE

20 to 200

LEVEL OF PHYSICAL ACTIVITY

High

ESTIMATED TIME

5 to 10 minutes

PROPS

None

To get participants up and moving, let them play Dominoes—using themselves as the Dominoes! Use this activity with groups that are willing to participate in a playful activity as an energizer, or with less playful types as an introduction to a more serious discussion of the domino effect.

INSTRUCTIONS

1. Organize participants into groups of ten to twenty people.
2. Explain the domino effect—situations that arise when one thing causes another to happen, which in turn causes something else, much like a row of falling dominoes each knocking over the next domino in turn.

3. Tell groups that they will each demonstrate the domino effect using the following procedures:

   - Groups will have 2 minutes to decide what formation to make and practice making it (from a standing position, one at a time bend down and then stand back up). They may choose a formation that requires more people than are in their own group.
   - With the rest of the group as audience, each group will then make the formation and behave as dominoes.

4. Instruct the groups to begin their strategizing.

5. After 2 minutes, ask each group, one at a time, to come to a visible position and create its formation. If a group needs more people, they may ask other groups to participate with them.

VARIATION

Ask each group to decide on a formation for the entire group to play out, and have the entire group do all of the formations.

TIPS

1. Bring dominoes and set them up. Then introduce the activity by pushing down the first domino and letting participants watch them all fall.

2. Encourage groups to make their formations as intricate as they dare.

28. MOTOR MANIA

PURPOSE

Complete Strangers; Team Building; Pure Fun; Outdoors; Stuffy, Conservative Types

GROUP SIZE

24 to 160

LEVEL OF PHYSICAL ACTIVITY

High

ESTIMATED TIME

10 to 20 minutes

PROPS

None

Participants will be on their feet and working together in this activity as they become the motorized objects of their choice. The activity is wonderful for culminating a program or inserting an achievement activity into team building! It always works. Groups love it, even engineers! (On second thought, particularly engineers.)

INSTRUCTIONS

1. Organize participants into groups of eight to sixteen.
2. Tell groups that they will have 5 minutes to truly become a motorized moving object, which means that each individual will physically participate in performing roles necessary

for the depiction of that object. Give examples, like a blender or fan.

3. Explain that at the end of 5 minutes, each group will demonstrate its object, while the other groups guess what object the group is portraying.

4. Give the signal to begin the planning time.

5. After 5 minutes, call on groups one at a time to demonstrate their motorized moving objects, while the other groups guess what the objects are. If no one guesses correctly, ask the performing group to reveal the motorized object they portrayed.

6. Encourage the other participants to applaud after each object is revealed.

VARIATIONS

1. Give the groups the names of the objects they should portray.

2. Give prizes for categories like synchronization, teamwork, and originality.

TIPS

1. This activity works best with open space.

2. Play upbeat music while participants are planning.

29. PECULIARITIES

PURPOSE

Sales Meetings; Complete Strangers; Pure Fun

GROUP SIZE

12 to 60

LEVEL OF PHYSICAL ACTIVITY

Low

ESTIMATED TIME

2 to 5 minutes

PROPS

Peculiarities Activity Sheet for leader; simple prizes such as candy, stickers, or pens

Peculiarities is a quick, light, and easy way for individuals to find out about one another. It may be used at any time during a short or long session, with participants who know one another well or with complete strangers, to introduce the topic of diversity. For long sessions, I recommend using a few examples every hour or so to inject interest and humor.

INSTRUCTIONS

1. Ask participants to stand.
2. Explain that the object of the activity is to discover peculiarities in the group.

3. Tell participants that you will read items from a list, one at a time. Ask them to come forward to receive a prize if they respond affirmatively to the category.

VARIATION

Pass out the list to participants and ask them to fill it out individually, then find others in the room who have marked the same categories. Include some categories that you know apply to more than one person.

TIPS

1. Keep this quick, light, and fun.
2. Add peculiarities to the list relating to organizational quirks or norms, or add specific peculiarities that you know about people in the group.

1. Was born on February 29.
2. Has or had a dog named Spot, Midnight, Lucky, or Shadow.
3. Is wearing an article of clothing that was chosen and purchased by someone else.
4. Is wearing a family heirloom.
5. Drives a car more than five years old.
6. Competes in sporting events such as running, skiing, etc.
7. Likes pizza with anchovies.
8. Volunteers for charity fund drives.
9. Was born in another state.
10. Was born in another country.
11. Has won a prize.
12. Has been to Idaho.
13. Writes songs or poetry.
14. Has an organized, clean desk.
15. Has a twin brother or sister.
16. Has a shoe size of 12 or greater.
17. Has milked a cow.
18. Has been to the top of the Washington Monument.
19. Collects stamps or other collectibles.
20. Remembers sodas for five cents.
21. Has been to a concert in the last month.
22. Has five or more siblings.
23. Prefers winter to summer.
24. Has been on a radio or TV show.
25. Restores old cars or trucks.
26. Has won a prize or money with a mail-in form.

30. POETRY IN MOTION

PURPOSE

Groups of 20 or More; Pure Fun; Outdoors

GROUP SIZE

20 to 60

LEVEL OF PHYSICAL ACTIVITY

High

ESTIMATED TIME

5 to 10 minutes

PROPS

Three to six poems (one per group) that would lend themselves to movement. An example is given on the Poetry in Motion Activity Sheet.

In this activity, participants find themselves enjoying movement and one another. Use it when you want people to have a break or just for sheer enjoyment.

INSTRUCTIONS

1. Organize participants into groups of eight to ten.
2. Give one poem to each group.
3. Explain that each piece of poetry has its own rhythm.
4. Tell participants they will have 5 minutes to a) decide on movements that will correspond to the reading of the poetry; and b) practice those movements to perform for the other groups.

5. After 5 minutes, ask each group to perform its movements to its poem.

1. Make this a contest with judging by a panel of participants.
2. Have people select their own poems from a variety that you supply.

1. Encourage large movements by providing plenty of space.
2. Ask participants to create props to accompany their performance.

The Charge of the Light Brigade

by Alfred, Lord Tennyson

Half a league, half a league,
Half a league onward,
All in the valley of Death
Rode the six hundred.
"Forward, the Light Brigade!
Charge for the guns!" he said:
Into the valley of Death
Rode the six hundred.

"Forward, the Light Brigade!"
Was there a man dismayed?
Not though the soldier knew
Some one had blundered.
Theirs not to make reply,
Theirs not to reason why,
Theirs but to do and die:
Into the valley of Death
Rode the six hundred.

Cannon to right of them,
Cannon to left of them,
Cannon in front of them
Volleyed and thundered;
Stormed at with shot and shell,
Boldly they rode and well,
Into the jaws of Death,
Into the mouth of Hell
Rode the six hundred.

Flashed all their sabers bare,
Flashed as they turned in air
Sabering the gunners there,
Charging an army, while
All the world wondered:
Plunged in the battery-smoke
Right through the line they broke;
Cossack and Russian
Reeled from the saber-stroke
Shattered and sundered.
Then they rode back, but not,
Not the six hundred.

Cannon to right of them,
Cannon to left of them,
Cannon behind them
Volleyed and thundered;
Stormed at with shot and shell,
While horse and hero fell,
They that had fought so well
Came through the jaws of Death
Back from the mouth of Hell,
All that was left of them,
Left of six hundred.

When can their glory fade?
O, the wild charge they made!
All the world wondered.
Honor the charge they made!
Honor the Light Brigade,
Noble six hundred!

Icebreakers for Introducing a Topic

31. ARRIVALS AND DEPARTURES

PURPOSE

Complete Strangers; Introducing a Topic; Stuffy, Conservative Types

GROUP SIZE

6 to 12

LEVEL OF PHYSICAL ACTIVITY

Low

ESTIMATED TIME

2 to 5 minutes

PROPS

Arrivals and Departures Activity Sheet

In Arrivals and Departures, participants list behaviors they would like to attain or get rid of. Use this activity at the beginning or end of a session in which people have been focusing on behavior change, either procedural or personal. This activity works very well in management and supervisory, communication, conflict, diversity, motivational, and personal effectiveness sessions.

INSTRUCTIONS

1. Copy the Arrivals and Departures Activity Sheet onto a transparency.
2. At the end of a session, put the transparency on the projector for everyone to see.

115

3. Explain that when we take personal responsibility for our own actions, we take the time to examine our own behaviors to decide whether to keep, modify, or change them to get the results we want.

4. Ask participants to consider the behaviors they choose to keep or would like to implement as arrivals, and the behaviors they would like to get rid of or change dramatically as departures.

5. Ask each person to talk with a person next to them about behaviors they have been in touch with during the session and identify at least one arrival and one departure that they are committed to working on.

VARIATION

If the group is small, ask each person to talk about arrivals and departures aloud.

TIP

Ask the group for stories about observations on arrivals and departures.

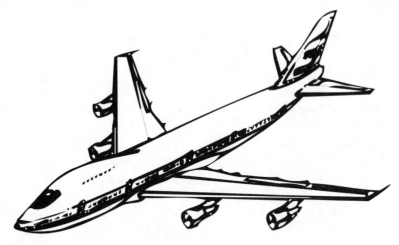

Departures

Arrivals

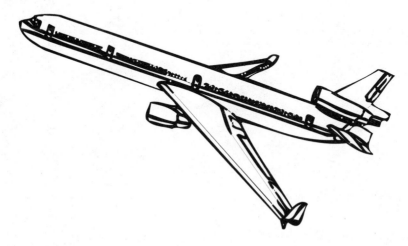

32. CONSTRUCTIVE FEEDBACK

PURPOSE

Introducing a Topic; Self-Disclosure; Stuffy, Conservative Types

GROUP SIZE

6 to 12

LEVEL OF PHYSICAL ACTIVITY

Medium

ESTIMATED TIME

3 to 6 minutes

PROPS

Box; 30 pieces of wadded paper

Your participants will value the benefits of constructive feedback as they try to accomplish a goal that is not possible without feedback from their peers. It works best with a small group of people who can all participate. Use it at any time in a program to introduce the value of feedback. Conceptual thinkers will make the most of the activity if you ask them to draw conclusions; concrete thinkers will appreciate the experiential demonstration.

INSTRUCTIONS

1. Ask for one volunteer.

2. When that person comes forward, position the volunteer in a standing position and place an empty cardboard box somewhere behind him or her, but not directly behind.

3. Place the 30 pieces of wadded paper within reach of the volunteer.

4. Explain to the group that their job is to give clues to the volunteer that will help him or her to throw the wads into the cardboard box without turning around. Give examples of clues such as, "A little further to the left."

5. Begin the activity.

6. About halfway through the activity, remind the volunteer of some of the clues given. Ask which ones were actually helpful and why that was true.

7. Keep the activity going until the volunteer has successfully thrown three wads into the cardboard box.

8. Ask the group to describe what is true about feedback based on what occurred in the exercise.

VARIATION

If you have fewer than seven people and more than 5 minutes, ask them all to stand in a square and do the activity for each person, one at a time.

TIP

Points to make if they don't come from the group:
- In this situation, feedback was expected and welcome.
- One person could not make the goal in a timely manner without hearing other perspectives and suggestions.
- When the goal was accomplished, everyone participated in enjoying the success.

33. IF I HAD A HAMMER

PURPOSE

Pure Fun; Introducing a Topic

GROUP SIZE

6 to 24

LEVEL OF PHYSICAL ACTIVITY

Medium

ESTIMATED TIME

3 to 5 minutes

PROPS

If I Had a Hammer Activity Sheet, one per participant

Participants compare the "tools" they learned about in the session to the drawings of real tools on an activity sheet. Use this activity to gain closure on an informative or skill-building session.

INSTRUCTIONS

1. Distribute one If I Had a Hammer Activity Sheet to each participant.
2. Ask participants to think of the tools they became acquainted with during the session.
3. Instruct them to make analogies between the tools on the sheet and the tools they heard about during the session.
4. When participants are finished, ask them to explain their analogies for each tool to the group.

1. Ask participants to list tools, then make analogies.
2. Create a sheet with a column of hardware tools next to a column of business tools and ask participants to match each hardware tool with a business tool, and then explain their matches.
3. Give each group one of the tools to create analogies for.
4. Use the tools for a grouping activity in the beginning of the session.

TIP

Bring in some tools to introduce the activity.

IF I HAD A HAMMER ACTIVITY SHEET

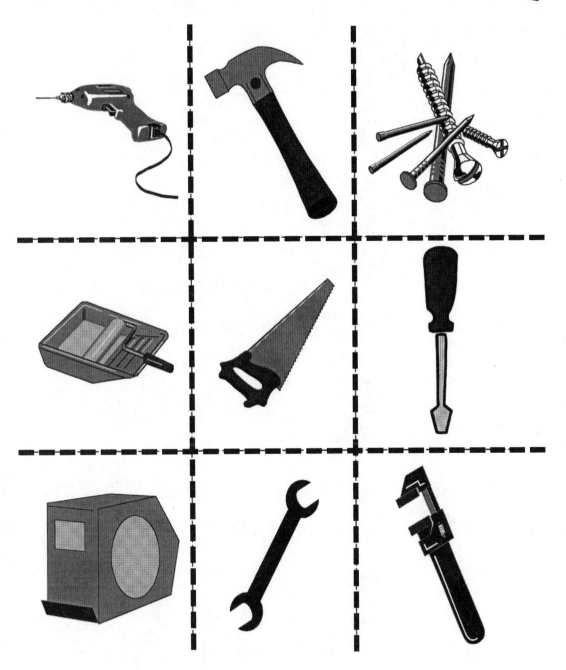

34. NATURE CALLS

PURPOSE

Team Building; Introducing a Topic; Stuffy, Conservative Types

GROUP SIZE

8 to 40

LEVEL OF PHYSICAL ACTIVITY

High

ESTIMATED TIME

25 to 35 minutes

PROPS

Nature Calls Activity Sheet, one per team

This is a special kind of scavenger hunt for teams. Instead of having a list of common items to find, teams must find items that most closely resemble the pictures of items on the sheet. This allows for some humor and creativity.

INSTRUCTIONS

1. Organize participants into teams of two to six.
2. Give each team a Nature Calls Activity Sheet.
3. Tell teams they have 20 minutes to find items that most closely resemble the pictures on the sheet.
4. Explain that when the 20 minutes are up, each team should bring its items to a central location for judging. Each item will be judged against the pictures. The winner of the com-

petition will be the team that has the greatest number of items that most closely resemble the pictures on the sheet.

VARIATION

Rather than using pictures from nature, use pictures of shapes or other objects.

TIPS

1. Encourage creativity for objects not easy to find.
2. Have first, second, third place with prizes for each.

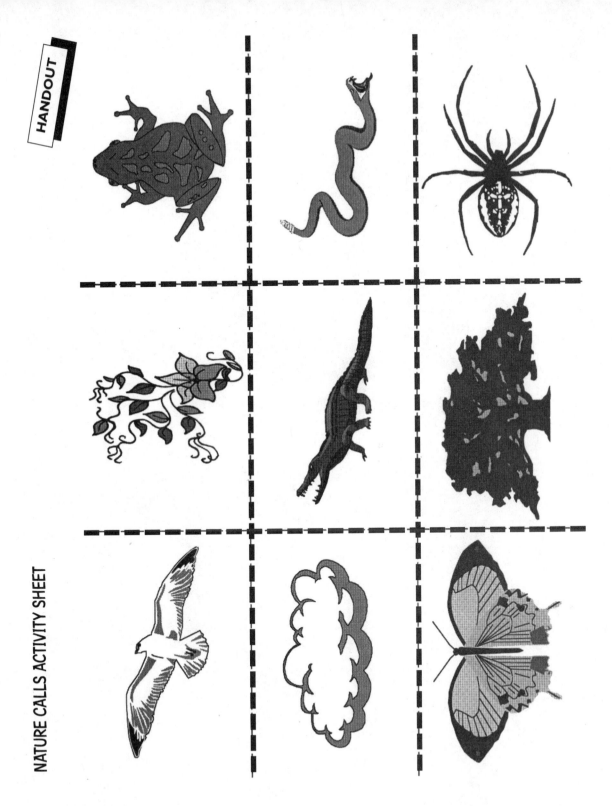

NATURE CALLS ACTIVITY SHEET

35. WARNING SIGNS

PURPOSE

Team Building; Introducing a Topic

GROUP SIZE

6 to 600

LEVEL OF PHYSICAL ACTIVITY

Medium

ESTIMATED TIME

3 to 5 minutes

PROPS

Warning Signs Activity Sheets, one per participant

A set of warning signs helps stimulate discussion as participants think of workplace analogies for each sign. Use this activity with supervisors, managers, and leaders to help them recognize their own strengths and limitations. It also works well for team building and conflict management because it helps people recognize pressure points—their own and others'. This is a light activity when used with a large group, but can become very self-disclosing when used with a more intimate group.

INSTRUCTIONS

1. Give each participant a Warning Signs Activity Sheet.
2. Tell them to take 2 minutes to write underneath each sign those work situations that correlate to the sign.

3. After 2 minutes, organize participants into pairs.

4. Ask them to share their signs and work situations with their partners.

VARIATIONS

1. Have participants work in groups and list all situations possible under each sign.

2. Have participants make the list a "Watch Out" list for themselves and use it as a closing activity.

TIP

Introduce the activity by giving examples of your own that fit the signs.

DANGER
CONFINED SPACE
ENTER BY
PERMIT ONLY

DANGER
DO NOT
DOUBLEDECK

DANGER
EXPLOSIVES

DANGER
HARD HAT
AREA

DANGER
LASER
OPERATING

DANGER
NO
ADMITTANCE

DANGER
NO PEDESTRIAN
TRAFFIC

DANGER
PINCH POINT

DANGER
DO NOT TRAVEL
WITH
FORKS RAISED

Icebreakers for Outdoors

36. ALL ABOARD

PURPOSE

Complete Strangers; Groups of 20 or More; Pure Fun; Outdoors

GROUP SIZE

20 to 100

LEVEL OF PHYSICAL ACTIVITY

High

ESTIMATED TIME

5 to 8 minutes

PROPS

Two balloons per person of varying colors (one color per group); one permanent magic marker per group of six to twenty

Participants will enjoy forming a "train" and picking up passengers. This activity encourages team behaviors and creativity. Use it when you have three to sixty minutes in open space when you want people to be very active.

INSTRUCTIONS

1. Distribute deflated balloons of varying colors around the space.
2. Organize participants into groups of six to twenty.
3. Ask groups to get into train formation and give each engine a magic marker.

4. Tell groups that they are passenger trains who must pick up passengers—2 passengers per car (per person).

5. Explain that balloons become passengers easily when one inflates them and creates a face on them with magic marker.

6. Tell them to move around in train formation to a location where there is a balloon. One person must inflate the balloon, tie it, and paint a face on it with magic marker. That person (or car) then carries that passenger with them. Each car will eventually be carrying two passengers in it.

7. Explain that groups will be competing to fill their trains (two passengers per car) with passengers of the same color. The train that is filled first wins the race.

8. Remind participants that their train must stay still while a person is inflating a balloon and drawing a face on it. The train can then move on to find another balloon (passenger) of like color. The only time trains can uncouple is when they are standing still.

VARIATIONS

1. Use pieces of cloth rather than balloons, increasing the pace of the race.

2. Tell groups they must have five or six different color balloons.

TIPS

1. Remind participants that they must have two passengers per person when they pull into the station.

2. Have everyone look at all the faces created.

37. IN SHAPE

PURPOSE

Groups of 20 or More; Pure Fun; Outdoors

GROUP SIZE

24 to 200

LEVEL OF PHYSICAL ACTIVITY

High

ESTIMATED TIME

5 to 10 minutes

PROPS

In Shape Activity Sheet for leader; numbered cards, one per group

Groups work together to form shapes in this high-energy activity. Use this as an energizer when you have adequate space with a group that appreciates a challenge and movement.

INSTRUCTIONS

1. Organize participants into groups of twelve to twenty.
2. Ask each group to name a leader and give each leader one large card with a number on it.
3. Explain that they will now be engaged in group competition. You will call out the name of a shape and each group should take on that shape.
4. Tell them to practice by forming a circle. Then ask them to form a square.

5. Explain that you will call shapes in rapid succession. As soon as a group has formed the shape, the group leader should hold up its number. You will call out the number of that group and then call out the next shape.

6. Explain that the object of the activity is for groups to score points by completing the shape first.

7. Begin the activity.

VARIATIONS

1. Allow each group to complete the shape before moving on.

2. If it's a well-educated group, use shapes like rhomboid or parallelogram.

TIPS

1. If you have a large group, make sure you're using a microphone or megaphone so that you can be heard over the din.

2. The more room there is, the freer groups feel about running around.

3. To decide how many shapes to call, sense the interest of the group.

IN SHAPE ACTIVITY SHEET (FOR THE LEADER)

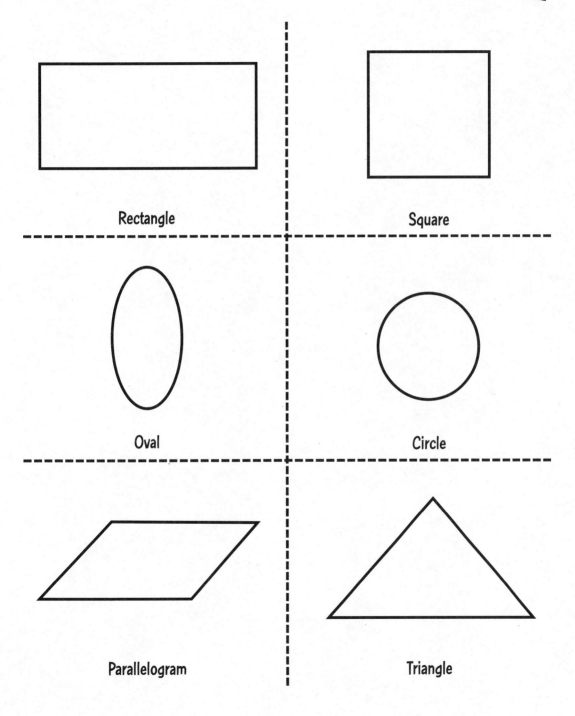

Rectangle

Square

Oval

Circle

Parallelogram

Triangle

38. POLYESTER TRIATHLON

PURPOSE

Sales Meetings; Groups of 20 or More; Outdoors; Self-Disclosure

GROUP SIZE

10 to 40

LEVEL OF PHYSICAL ACTIVITY

High

ESTIMATED TIME

5 minutes each time

PROPS

Polyester Triathlon Activity Sheet

This activity gives participants who might never qualify for a triathlon the chance to experience one—and a creative one at that. Because groups design their own physical activities, it doesn't matter whether you have lots of open space or not.

INSTRUCTIONS

1. Organize participants into three groups.
2. Explain that they will be participating in a relay race called Polyester Triathlon.
3. Tell each group they have 2 minutes to choose an event to include in the triathlon. Encourage creativity. (Examples might include running in place for a count of 100; walking backward from one specific location to another; singing

"Yankee Doodle" while riding an imaginary horse around a circle; turning around in circles 10 times; and so on.)

4. After 2 minutes, ask each group in turn to perform the event it selected. Then ask all participants to practice that move.

5. Tell groups to line up in the order in which they will perform the triathlon.

6. Explain that you will blow the whistle and the triathlon will begin. Each person in a group must perform all three of the events decided upon by all groups, and then the next person in the group begins. The group that finishes first wins.

7. Following the competition, distribute Polyester Triathlon medals.

VARIATIONS

1. Make it an individual competition.

2. Give the groups the events they should complete.

3. Conduct this activity indoors and ask participants to choose pretend events, such as swimming in a swamp of alligators.

TIP

Use fun props such as a sign that says Starting Line, water bottles, or sweatbands.

POLYESTER TRIATHLON ACTIVITY SHEET

39. RIDE 'EM, COWBOY

PURPOSE

Groups of 20 or More; Pure Fun; Outdoors

GROUP SIZE

20 to 200

LEVEL OF PHYSICAL ACTIVITY

High

ESTIMATED TIME

10 to 30 minutes

PROPS

Ride 'em, Cowboy cards, one event per group, one card per participant; lively music

This high-energy activity gives each group a chance to entertain the rest of the participants. Use this activity midway through or at the end of a program; participants will be less inhibited in their performances after spending some time together.

INSTRUCTIONS

1. Organize participants into groups of five to twenty.
2. Give each group cards for each person. Explain that each group has the name of a different event that may occur at a rodeo.

3. Explain that groups will have 5 minutes to develop and practice the events shown on their card before performing them for the whole group at "show time."

4. Give the signal to begin planning and practicing.

5. After 5 minutes, ask the groups to take turns performing their acts in the center of the room.

VARIATIONS

1. Ask groups to come up with their own events.

2. Give all groups the same events.

3. At the end, call for work analogies (e.g., Riding the bucking bronco is like. . .).

TIPS

1. This is your chance to a run a rodeo. Enjoy it!

2. Encourage groups to applaud for each performance.

Calf Roping

Hog Tying

Bull Riding

Bareback Riding

40. THE WAVES

PURPOSE

Complete Strangers; Groups of 20 or More; Outdoors

GROUP SIZE

15 to 100

LEVEL OF PHYSICAL ACTIVITY

High

ESTIMATED TIME

3 to 5 minutes

PROPS

None

Many people have experienced the wave—that uplifted arm movement that moves through stadium crowds like a wave crashing on water—so this appeals to all audiences. It is a great energizer, outdoors or indoors, and may become as elaborate as you dare to make it.

INSTRUCTIONS

1. Organize participants standing in a semicircle with everyone facing in and you standing at one end.
2. Demonstrate the typical wave by throwing your arms up and asking the person next to you to follow, and so on, all the way down the line, with the last person bringing his or her arms down, at which point all participants in turn put their arms down until it is back to you.

3. Explain that there are many types of waves.

4. Ask them to follow with the same wave pattern each time you lead.

5. Lead them by taking one step to the right while throwing your arms over your head and to the right.

6. When that wave comes back to you, take two fast steps forward while throwing your arms forward.

7. When that wave comes back to you, spin around on one foot 180° and stand facing in the opposite direction.

8. Continue the activity with any other version of the wave you can think of. The rest is up to you. Have fun!

VARIATIONS

1. Ask a participant to be the leader, or have participants take turns leading.

2. If participants are dressed appropriately, perform waves from a sitting or lying position.

TIP

Have great fun with this: laugh with the mistakes, increase the speed, and perform outrageous moves.

Icebreakers for Self-Disclosure

41. HAPPY BIRTHDAY!

PURPOSE

Groups of 20 or More; Pure Fun; Self-Disclosure

GROUP SIZE

20 to 200

LEVEL OF PHYSICAL ACTIVITY

High

ESTIMATED TIME

3 to 6 minutes

PROPS

None

This activity brings together people born in the same month, and possibly on the same day. It works every time, even with people who have done it before. Use this activity with any group; age and group size don't matter.

INSTRUCTIONS

1. Explain the importance of celebrating birthdays, remembering and valuing an individual just for existing.
2. Ask participants to walk around and find others who share the same birth month. For example, my birthday is in September, so I would walk around yelling "September" until I find others with the same birthday.
3. When participants are in birth month groups, ask them to yell out their months in order, beginning with January.

4. Then ask group members to share their exact birth dates.

5. Ask how many people discovered common birth dates.

VARIATION

Ask month groups to plan for and then demonstrate, rather than yell out, their months. For example, the May group might act out dancing around a maypole.

TIP

Keep this activity crisp, quick, light, and fun.

42. KEY TO MY HEART

PURPOSE

Team Building; Pure Fun; Self-Disclosure

GROUP SIZE

4 to 40

LEVEL OF PHYSICAL ACTIVITY

Low

ESTIMATED TIME

8 to 10 minutes

PROPS

Key to My Heart Activity Sheet, one per participant

This activity gives participants the opportunity to learn something personal and meaningful about each other.

INSTRUCTIONS

1. Organize participants into groups of three to six.
2. Ask participants to each choose one key they have with them that opens the path to things or persons most close to their hearts.
3. Tell them to complete the Key to My Heart Activity Sheets.
4. Tell them they have 5 minutes in their groups to use the information on their sheets to share with one another their keys and pathways to the heart.

VARIATIONS

1. Organize participants into pairs; ask them to tell one another a heart-wrenching story; then ask each person to share the partner's heart-wrenching story with group members.

2. Ask each participant to put a key in the middle of the table. Ask each group member to create a heart-wrenching story for that person and tell it to the rest of the group.

TIPS

1. People will only reveal what they choose to reveal.
2. Begin with your own heart-wrenching story.

KEY TO MY HEART ACTIVITY SHEET

This activity will give you a chance to share with others a heartfelt experience or situation.

1. Choose a key from your key ring that has heartfelt meaning for you.

2. In the space below, write a few sentences that explain the meaning related to the key to your heart.

3. In the space below, make notes about a true story that comes from the reminder of the key to your heart.

4. Choose a partner and swap stories. If it is helpful, take notes about your partner's story in the space below.

5. Be prepared to tell your partner's Key to My Heart story to the rest of the group.

43. MOST LIKE ME

PURPOSE

Complete Strangers; Team Building; Self-Disclosure

GROUP SIZE

10 to 100

LEVEL OF PHYSICAL ACTIVITY

Low

ESTIMATED TIME

3 to 5 minutes

PROPS

Most Like Me Activity Sheets, one per participant

Participants compare themselves to characters in humorous illustrations as a way of finding out more about one another. This activity works well for any group to get to know one another, to find out more about one another, or to encourage self-disclosure.

INSTRUCTIONS

1. Distribute Most Like Me Activity Sheets to participants.
2. Ask them to look at the pictures on the sheet and place an X in the corners of the pictures that are most like them.
3. When they've selected, ask them to form triads and share with those people the selections they've made and why they chose them.

VARIATION

Ask groups or a team to make a composite sheet of everyone in the group and share that sheet with other groups.

TIP

If your group is small, ask participants to share with the total group.

MOST LIKE ME ACTIVITY SHEET

44. STRIKING RESEMBLANCE

PURPOSE

Team Building; Outdoors; Self-Disclosure

GROUP SIZE

6 to 30

LEVEL OF PHYSICAL ACTIVITY

Low

ESTIMATED TIME

8 to 10 minutes

PROPS

Striking Resemblance Activity Sheets, one per participant

The expression "behaving like an animal," is not too great a stretch from reality. In this activity, participants reveal their usual ways of reacting to certain types of situations. They will have fun with this one.

INSTRUCTIONS

1. Organize participants into groups of four to six.
2. Give each person one Striking Resemblance Activity Sheet.
3. Give them 5 minutes to complete the sheet.
4. Tell them to share their responses in their groups.
5. When they're finished, ask them to share observations about the exercise with the total group.

VARIATIONS

1. If the group is small, ask them to share responses with all participants.
2. Ask participants to add to the list of questions and complete them.

TIP

Keep this activity light.

Choose from the following pictures to fill in the blanks.

1. When I find that things aren't getting done in the time I would like to see them done, I behave most like a(n) _____.

2. When things are sailing along nicely, I behave most like a(n) _____.

3. When I appear to disagree with most of my coworkers, I behave most like a(n) _____.

4. When I am in charge of a project, I behave most like a(n) _____.

5. When I have a project to do that I don't like, I behave most like a(n) _____.

6. When I am working on my pet project, I behave most like a(n) _____.

7. When I am working well in a team environment, I behave most like a(n) _____.

8. When I disagree with the direction in which the organization is heading, I behave most like a(n) _____.

9. When I see a goal clearly and am inspired to head toward it, I behave most like a(n) _____.

10. When I work alone, I behave most like a(n) _____.

11. I prefer most to behave like a(n) _____.

12. I prefer least to behave like a(n) _____.

45. THE COLOR OF LOVE

PURPOSE

Complete Strangers; Self-Disclosure; Team Building

GROUP SIZE

8 to 28

LEVEL OF PHYSICAL ACTIVITY

Low

ESTIMATED TIME

5 to 7 minutes

PROPS

Color of Love Activity Sheets, one per participant

Colors evoke emotional responses differently in different people. This activity is a fun way for participants to hear how people think "in color."

INSTRUCTIONS

1. Give one Color of Love Activity Sheet to each person.
2. Tell participants they have 2 minutes to complete the sheets.
3. After 2 minutes, ask participants to organize into groups of three.
4. Tell participants to share their answers with the other two individuals in their groups.

If the group is small, have everyone share their answers.

TIPS

1. Have color templates around the room or on the table.
2. Play on the "colorfulness" of the group.

THE COLOR OF LOVE ACTIVITY SHEET

Answer the following questions with the name of a color.

1. What color is happiness?

2. What color is sadness?

3. What color is tenderness?

4. What color is loneliness?

5. What color is friskiness?

6. What color is creativity?

7. What color is intelligence?

8. What color is love?

9. What is your favorite color?

10. What is your least favorite color?

Icebreakers for Stuffy, Conservative Types Who Hate Icebreakers

46. CONTINUOUS IMPROVEMENT

PURPOSE

Staff Meetings; Sales Meetings; Stuffy, Conservative Types Who Hate Icebreakers

GROUP SIZE

6 to 20

LEVEL OF PHYSICAL ACTIVITY

Low

ESTIMATED TIME

3 to 6 minutes

PROPS

Flip chart or board with the letters A, B, C, and D

There's a tendency to blame the leader for the success of meetings. In the spirit of ongoing continuous improvement, this activity allows participants to monitor their own meeting and contributing behaviors. Use this when you suspect that people are not aware of the results of their behaviors, or when you want the group to recognize progress.

INSTRUCTIONS

1. Toward the end of a meeting, show participants the flip chart or board.
2. Explain that participants will now have an opportunity to evaluate their own meeting behaviors.

3. Ask participants to choose two of their own behaviors during the meeting, and mentally rate themselves with two letter grades, from A to D.

4. Ask each person to share the self-ratings with the other participants.

5. If it seems appropriate, allow for reactions from other participants.

VARIATIONS

1. Have participants rate items on the agenda instead.
2. Ask table groups to discuss their answers.

TIPS

1. You might begin the session by asking participants to identify good and bad meeting behaviors.
2. Send the responses back out to people with the meeting notes, so they will be more conscious of their behavior the next time.

47. PHOBIA MANIA

PURPOSE

Complete Strangers; Pure Fun; Stuffy, Conservative Types

GROUP SIZE

10 to 40

LEVEL OF PHYSICAL ACTIVITY

Low

ESTIMATED TIME

5 to 7 minutes

PROPS

Flip chart paper and markers for each group

In this activity participants confront and name their true fears—those never named before—in a humorous way. It is best used as a mental and emotional energizer anytime during a program or as an introduction to fears about of your topic, such as organizational change.

INSTRUCTIONS

1. Organize participants into groups of three to five.
2. Explain that there are currently many named phobias, but there must be a few that have yet to be discovered.
3. Give examples of phobias and ask for a show of hands for each phobia participants have heard of.

4. Explain that they will now have 3 minutes with their groups to list and create names for phobias never before named. Provide an example, such as "Grasspest phobia: the fear of walking barefoot on grass and being stung by a bee hidden in the long blades."

5. Instruct groups to write their phobias with definitions on flip chart paper.

6. When the 3 minutes are up, ask each group to report its phobias and definitions.

VARIATIONS

1. Ask groups to choose one phobia and illustrate it before sharing it with the group.

2. Use work phobias as the topic for participants to work within.

TIPS

1. Keep it light; this isn't a therapy session.

2. Don't make fun of real fears that people suffer from.

3. Examples of phobias: acrophobia—fear of heights; claustrophobia—fear of enclosed spaces; arachnophobia—fear of spiders.

48. ROAD SIGNS

PURPOSE

Sales Meetings; Introducing a Topic; Stuffy, Conservative Types

GROUP SIZE

6 to 30

LEVEL OF PHYSICAL ACTIVITY

Medium

ESTIMATED TIME

3 to 5 minutes

PROPS

Road Signs Activity Sheets, one per participant

Use this activity with groups that would enjoy working with analogies; they'll be pairing common road signs to life on the job. Engineers, middle managers, marketing personnel, and executives are examples of groups that fit into this category.

INSTRUCTIONS

1. Give each person a Road Sign Activity Sheet.
2. Instruct participants to look at the road signs and think of analogies to the organization that help or discourage them from reaching their goals. Give examples, such as: Detour—Sometimes we're moving along well, and suddenly we come upon a situation for which we must deviate from our current strategies; or Max Height 12'6"—We like to

know the parameters before we proceed so we don't get halfway there and have to stop.

3. When people are finished, ask them to share their analogies aloud.

VARIATIONS

1. Give each group one road sign and ask them to come up with an analogy for it.

2. Give each group all road signs and see what different analogies the different groups come up with. Use them periodically throughout the session.

TIP

If you use this activity early in a session, chances are good that participants will keep referring back to the analogies, or will name new ones that relate to other organizational situations.

ROAD SIGN ACTIVITY SHEET

49. TIDDLYWINKS

PURPOSE

Staff Meetings; Introducing a Topic; Stuffy, Conservative Types

GROUP SIZE

6 to 12

LEVEL OF PHYSICAL ACTIVITY

Medium

ESTIMATED TIME

2 to 5 minutes

PROPS

Tiddlywinks (5 per person); Tiddlywinks Competition Chart; a bowl or basket

This activity is a way to generate smiles and bring participants to the table on time. Use it for regularly scheduled meetings as a motivator for on-time attendance.

INSTRUCTIONS

1. Create a Tiddlywinks Competition Chart to keep with you when coming to meetings.
2. At each meeting, distribute 5 tiddlywinks to each person.
3. Put a bowl or basket in the middle of the table the group will be using.
4. Tell participants to put their tiddlywinks the length of one spread hand from the edge of the table in front of them.

5. Explain that the object of the activity is to use one of the tiddlywinks to shoot the others into the basket. For each one that goes in the basket, the shooter scores one point.

6. Explain that you will keep track of points from meeting to meeting, and at every fourth meeting you'll announce a winner.

VARIATIONS

1. If you don't have tiddlywinks, have participants toss pieces of foam into a cup.

2. Organize the group into teams and have teams complete.

TIPS

1. Tiddlywinks are fun to use because most people have heard the name, but few have actually played with them.

2. This activity should be purely for fun.

50. YOU ARE WHAT YOU READ

PURPOSE

Staff Meetings; Self-Disclosure; Stuffy, Conservative Types

GROUP SIZE

5 to 150

LEVEL OF PHYSICAL ACTIVITY

Low

ESTIMATED TIME

5 to 10 minutes

PROPS

None

This activity is good for any type of audience, including upper management types, because everyone enjoys sharing information. The beginning of the program is a great time to use it, although it works at any time.

INSTRUCTIONS

1. Organize participants into groups of two to ten.
2. Ask participants to write down the books or magazines they have read most recently, say in the last two weeks.
3. Invite one person in each group to be the Bookworm. The other participants in the group guess what kind of reading material the person wrote down.

4. Explain that once everyone in the group has given their opinions, the Bookworms reveal the kind of reading material they wrote down and explain why they read that material.

5. Remind groups to allow the opportunity for each person in the group to be the Bookworm.

VARIATION

Organize participants by like reading material and instruct them to collectively decide and then explain to the rest of the group why they read that type. Use categories like sports magazines, mysteries, autobiographies, etc.

TIPS

1. At break time, listen for such comments as, "So, how did you like *The Apostle?*"

2. This activity is often a leveler for groups of males and females, because each group relates to common topics.

Icebreakers While Waiting to Start

51. BRIEFCASE STICKERS

PURPOSE

Waiting to Start

GROUP SIZE

8 to 60

LEVEL OF PHYSICAL ACTIVITY

Low

ESTIMATED TIME

5 to 10 minutes

PROPS

Briefcase Sticker Activity Sheet, one per participant

In this activity, participants will have fun creating and then sharing stickers they would put on their briefcases that would let people at work know about something they think or believe.

INSTRUCTIONS

1. Organize participants into groups of 4 to 8.
2. Give each person a Briefcase Sticker Activity Sheet.
3. Explain that briefcase stickers are like bumper stickers, only without the wheels for them to ride on.
4. Ask them for examples of bumper stickers they've seen. Have some of your own ready in case they don't have many.

5. Tell them you know they have been anxious to create their own stickers for their briefcases; therefore, in their groups they'll have 5 minutes to collectively come up with a list of them.

6. Explain that after the group has come up with a list of them, each person in a group should select the one he or she wants, and puts it on their briefcase on the Briefcase Sticker Activity Sheet to show the other participants.

7. After 5 minutes, ask each group to stand and display and say their briefcase stickers for all participants.

VARIATIONS

1. Have each participant design their own.

2. Ask each person to design a briefcase sticker based on an experience they had at work recently.

TIPS

1. Keep this fun and light.

2. If the session is long enough, display these on a wall or board.

BRIEFCASE BUMPER ACTIVITY SHEET

Design your Briefcase Sticker on the briefcase below.

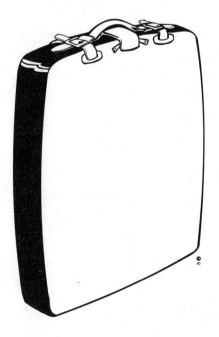

52. NEWS AND VIEWS

PURPOSE

> Waiting to Start

GROUP SIZE

> 6 to 300

LEVEL OF PHYSICAL ACTIVITY

> Low

ESTIMATED TIME

> 10 to 15 minutes

PROPS

> News articles from local or national paper for leader examples
>
> Next to the weather or available food, news events stir the greatest amount of conversation. This activity will allow people to share current events-and, more importantly, to give their own opinions about them.

INSTRUCTIONS

1. Organize participants into groups of 3 people.
2. Tell them that most people have a chance to read the paper or hear news each day. For some, the news is essential for business or personal interests; for others, humorous, interesting or fascinating; still for others, it may be discouraging.

3. Read to the group some news article of the day that was humorous or interesting for you.

4. Tell groups they have 10 minutes to talk about the events of the day, and share their own opinions regarding those events. Remind them to avoid getting into highly controversial issues since they often require more time than is available.

5. After 10 minutes, ask the total group if there were any stories of particular interest or discussion.

VARIATIONS

1. Give examples of news of the day, and ask them to discuss those you've related to them.

2. Ask them to discuss current events of the year or decade.

TIPS

1. Keep this activity light and objective.

2. Allow more time if participants are really getting into the activity.

53. WHAT WOULD YOU DO?

PURPOSE

Waiting to Start

GROUP SIZE

4 to 20

LEVEL OF PHYSICAL ACTIVITY

Low

ESTIMATED TIME

5 to 7 minutes

PROPS

One or two articles about people who dealt with difficult or humorous situations in a business setting for leader examples

People respond so differently to news of all types at work. This activity will allow participants to hear about how other people would react to situations that they may have reacted to themselves.

INSTRUCTIONS

1. Organize participants into groups of 2 to 4 people.
2. Read an article about a current situation, and one person's way of reacting to that situation (e.g. business merger). Explain that people often face new or shocking news in business situations. As a result, they tend to deal with the news in a variety of ways.

3. Tell groups they will have about 5 minutes to discuss similar situations they may have faced, and talk about ways they observed others dealing with, dealt with themselves, or would deal with themselves if they faced similar situations.

4. After 5 minutes, ask the total group if there were any stories of particular interest or discussion.

VARIATION

Have each person answer the What would you do? question for one or two specific situations.

TIP

Works best with a small group.

54. IN-BASKET

PURPOSE

Waiting to Start

GROUP SIZE

8 to 60

LEVEL OF PHYSICAL ACTIVITY

Low

ESTIMATED TIME

4 to 8 minutes

PROPS

In-basket Activity Sheet, one per participant

As people wait for a program to begin, their minds fill with the progress they could be making back on the job. During this activity, participants will be able to verbalize these anxieties, think through some possible actions or solutions, and hear what responsibilities other people have on the job.

INSTRUCTIONS

1. Ask each person to complete the In-basket Activity Sheet, noting the projects or tasks they're involved in that are of highest priority for the organization or for them.
2. Organize participants into groups of 2 to 6 people.
3. Tell participants they will have 4 minutes (or longer, if you wish) to share with one another what is on their In-basket

Activity Sheets, thereby explaining some of the work they do with one another.

4. Explain to participants that this is a great time to commiserate or get ideas from other people.

5. After 4 minutes (or longer), move on to the next activity or topic. This is one activity that needs no further discussion or questioning.

VARIATIONS

1. If the group is a current workgroup, you may want to facilitate a 10 minute discussion in their groups about ways they could support one another.

2. Ask participants to describe what is in their in-baskets on a daily basis.

TIPS

1. This needs little leader interaction. Just let them talk. Don't allow the session to become a teambuilding or therapy session unless that is the purpose of the program.

2. If the group is a current work group, encourage them to share their greatest concerns about their projects and activities.

IN-BASKET ACTIVITY SHEET

Many times when we come to a meeting, our minds are filled with the kinds of activities we would be engaged in if we are at work. At times we're pleased that we don't have to face the work; other times we're frustrated that we can't be there accomplishing things.

Here's an opportunity to think through the activities and projects we have in our in-baskets for the day.

Current activities and projects that I am currently engaged in that are a high priority for the organization:

1. _____
2. _____
3. _____
4. _____
5. _____

Current activities and projects that I am currently engaged in that are a high priority for me:

1. _____
2. _____
3. _____
4. _____
5. _____

What I would be doing today if I weren't at this meeting:

1. _____
2. _____
3. _____
4. _____
5. _____

Often in a meeting like this there are other people who are working on projects that have a professional or personal interest to you. You may even find people that you would like to connect with after the meeting.

Projects other people are engaged in that are of particular interest to me:

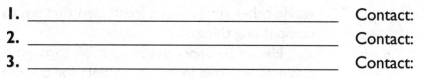

1. _____   Contact:
2. _____   Contact:
3. _____   Contact:

55. STARTING OVER...

PURPOSE

>Waiting to Start

GROUP SIZE

>8 to 60

LEVEL OF PHYSICAL ACTIVITY

>Low

ESTIMATED TIME

>5 to 10 minutes

PROPS

>Inspirational story of a person who overcame significant odds to achieve something great for the leader

INSTRUCTIONS

1. Tell participants a current inspirational story about a person who has overcome great odds (either personal or organizational) to achieve something great.

2. Explain that most of us have experienced a time in our lives when we were seemingly "starting over." This time may have been the result of a major life change such as a career decision or change, a significant event such as the birth of a child, or other personal change.

3. Organize participants into groups of 2 to 4 people.

4. Tell participants they will have 5 minutes to share their own "starting over" stories or other stories they know about. Ask participants to identify the story they found

most inspirational and why—talking about and identifying the character traits that helped the people they talked about make "starting over" a positive experience.

5. After 5 minutes, ask groups to share one of their most inspirational stories, and the character traits they thought were essential in making the "starting over" a positive experience.

VARIATIONS

1. Ask people to talk only about someone they knew who had to "start over."

2. Tell participants to identify the people who gave support to the person who had to start over, and ask them to give examples of times they were able to support someone who was starting over.

TIPS

1. This is a particularly powerful activity if the meeting or training program is about a significant change they or others in the organization will be experiencing in the near future.

2. Keep this light or serious, depending on the tone you want to create.

Icebreakers for
Everyday Living

56. THE NUMBERS GAME

PURPOSE

Everyday Living

GROUP SIZE

4 to 400

LEVEL OF PHYSICAL ACTIVITY

Low

ESTIMATED TIME

3 to 6 minutes

PROPS

None

In this activity, participants will be able to demonstrate their own proficiency with remembering multiple phone, fax and identification numbers; or they will get to vent their frustration with not being able to remember all the numbers and addresses of the day.

INSTRUCTIONS

1. Tell participants about a personal experience you had with trying to remember a cell phone number, or fax number, or a similar time experienced by someone you know. If you want, use my story about a day I listened patiently while a very frustrated person on the other end of the phone attempted to remember his apartment phone number. He had already listed his cell phone, two office phone numbers, and two fax numbers for me. The frustration was for

a society numbering itself so fast, individuals could not keep pace. I concluded that we live in an age of number addition-adding to our routine lists of birth dates, home phone numbers, house numbers, route numbers, anniversary dates, and social security numbers—fax numbers, cell phone numbers, phone card numbers, security identification numbers, and so on.

2. Explain to participants that this activity is a competitive activity. People will be competing for the honor of being Number 1, or for being the person "whose days are mostly numbered." They will be sharing these numbers for confirmation within.

3. Pass out or ask people to take out a blank sheet of paper.

4. Tell them they have 1 minute to list all the numbers they can think of.

5. After 1 minute, tell participants to share in their groups the numbers they have listed, and figure out who has the most (legitimate) numbers listed in the group. Humorously, encourage people in the groups to test legitimacy of the numbers anyway they can.

6. After groups have finished, ask each group to report the person in the group who had the most numbers.

7. After all groups have reported, name the winner of the Numbers Game-the individual who could name the most remembered numbers.

VARIATIONS

1. Have the competition occur between groups; each group adds all the numbers of the group and reports the total.

2. Use email addresses in place of numbers.

TIPS

1. This activity is purely for fun. Keep it very light.

2. Ask individuals who win to what do they attribute their success.

57. BIGGEST DEAL

PURPOSE

Everyday Living

GROUP SIZE

6 to 12

LEVEL OF PHYSICAL ACTIVITY

Low

ESTIMATED TIME

5 to 10 minutes

PROPS

Biggest Deal Activity Sheet, one per participant with optional crayons, markers, pens, colored pencils, or the like; sample Leader Biggest Deal Activity Sheet

We live in an age of discounts, off-price, and garage sale consumer negotiations. In this activity participants will get to use their creative juices to brag about bargains they received, and hear of others' bargains (although, no one really cares about someone else's savings).

INSTRUCTIONS

1. Tell the group about a time you got a real bargain. (If you have an object to bring in and talk about, that's even better.)
2. Show participants the Biggest Deal Activity Sheet you drew to illustrate your "biggest deal."

3. Distribute a Bigger Deal Activity Sheet to each participant.

4. Tell participants they have 3 minutes to think of the biggest deal they got, and to draw a picture of what that represented to them.

5. After 3 minutes, ask each participant to show their picture and describe their biggest deal.

6. When all have finished, ask the group to vote for the person they think got the "biggest deal" in the room.

VARIATIONS

1. With a larger group, organize participants into groups of 4 to 6. Ask each group to nominate their "Biggest Deal." Then use those people as leaders for another activity.

2. Ask groups to hear stories of negotiation and determine who in the group is the best haggler.

TIPS

1. Have fun with this; use story-telling license in the telling of your own story so it encourages participants to do the same.

2. This is a fun after-lunch activity for an all-day activity. Tee up the activity by saying that at lunchtime you were talking with someone who...

BIGGEST DEAL ACTIVITY SHEET

In the space provided below, please illustrate your biggest deal. Use shape, motion, color, and anything else available to make the impression that you really got the "biggest deal."

58. SOUNDS OF THE SURF

PURPOSE

Everyday Living

GROUP SIZE

10 to 50

LEVEL OF PHYSICAL ACTIVITY

Low

ESTIMATED TIME

5 to 10 minutes

PROPS

None

Each of us has an internal sound chamber where sounds reverberate and stimulate ideas, emotions, and thought patterns (or is it all thought patterns that then stimulate ideas and emotions?). In this activity participants learn about one another's unique ability to simulate ordinary sounds from their environments.

INSTRUCTIONS

1. Organize participants into groups of 6 to 10.
2. Explain the _____-like way of communicating sounds.
3. Tell groups they will now have 5 minutes to play a guessing game that involves each one of them in turn imitating a

particular sound (examples: the ocean, a machine, seagulls, radio static, etc.).

4. The rest of the group then gets 10 seconds to guess what the sound is simulating. During the 10 seconds, the individual may repeat the sound as many times as necessary.

5. After 10 seconds, if the group hasn't guessed the sound, play moves on to the next person.

6. At the end of 5 minutes, ask each group how many sounds they guessed, and for one person in the group to give a total group demonstration.

VARIATIONS

1. Limit the sounds to one topic, such as those of vacation spots or workplace settings.

2. If a small group, have each person demonstrate a sound while the rest of the group guesses.

TIPS

1. Play a tape of sounds prior to or during an explanation of the activity.

2. Don't use with groups that have an individual with significant hearing impairment.

59. RETURN ON INVESTMENT

PURPOSE

Everyday Living

GROUP SIZE

8 to 100

LEVEL OF PHYSICAL ACTIVITY

Medium

ESTIMATED TIME

3 to 6 minutes

PROPS

1 note card per participant; leader samples of mailings from charities

Most people give time or money to charitable organizations. In this activity, participants will learn the wide variety of organizations to which people contribute.

INSTRUCTIONS

1. Ask participants to stand with a paper and writing instrument in their hands. Explain that they will be gathering and writing down information from one another.
2. Talk about some local charity drive that is going on.
3. Explain that they are going to be hearing from each other about Returns On Investment which have nothing whatsoever to do with their careers or business endeavors. Share with them that there are so many worthy charitable

organizations, it is sometimes difficult to make decisions about where to put time and financial resources. Hold up and name mailings from charitable organizations. Explain that some people give to one or two, whereas other people spread their time or money over many charities.

4. Tell participants they will have 2 minutes to walk around asking each participant for the name of one of their favorite charities to which they contribute either time or money, and to list that the organization name on their note card. If a charity is already listed, they should not put it down again, but ask the person if they have another charity to list.

5. After 2 minutes, ask participants to call out names of charities, while you record them on a flip chart or computer screen. Explain that in addition to the value they each add to their employers' ROI, they add a great value to the bottom line of a society that cares about the needs of others.

VARIATIONS

1. Give them a list of charitable organizations and ask them to check each time they talk with a person who contributes to each one.

2. Organize participants into groups. Ask each person to make a pitch for their favorite charity. When they've finished, tally the list of charities.

TIPS

1. Use this activity as a way for people to encourage one another in their volunteer efforts.

2. This can be a fun or serious activity, depending on your purpose and the tone you set.

60. BORN ON THE ...

PURPOSE

Waiting to Start

GROUP SIZE

4 to 400

LEVEL OF PHYSICAL ACTIVITY

Low

ESTIMATED TIME

5 to 8 minutes

PROPS

Born On the... Activity Sheet for all participants

Since everyone has a birthday, this activity will give participants much to talk about.

INSTRUCTIONS

1. Give participants Born On the... Activity Sheets.
2. Organize participants into pairs.
3. Tell participants they have will each have 4 minutes to talk about the day/month/year they were born.
4. After 4 minutes, ask the total group, "How many of you pairs had the same year, month, or day?"
5. After responses, ask (humorously) of those who responded positively, "Did you notice any similarities between you because of that coincidence?"
6. Ask if there were any other interesting facts any of them would like to reveal.

1. Ask participants to work in groups of 4 to 6.
2. Have them fill out the sheet rather than just verbally answer the questions. addressed.

TIPS

1. If you've already used the Happy Birthday! Icebreaker, just focus on the details of the dates.
2. Start out by revealing your birth date, and something humorous related to that month or year.

BORN ON THE... ACTIVITY SHEET

Here are conversation starters related to your birthday.

1. What world events were occurring the year of your birth?

2. When you were a child, what did you like and not like about the month of your birthday?

3. What fond memories do you have of particular birthdays?

4. What do you like most and least about being your current age?

5. What age was the best for you?

Icebreakers for the Super Intelligent

61. PREDICTIONS

PURPOSE

Super Intelligent

GROUP SIZE

6 to 40

LEVEL OF PHYSICAL ACTIVITY

Low

ESTIMATED TIME

6 to 10 minutes

PROPS

Predictions Activity Sheet, one per participant

In this activity participants will get to hear the predictions from other people about a variety of topics of interest to them.

INSTRUCTIONS

1. Organize participants into groups of 4 to 5.
2. Distribute a Predictions Activity Sheet to each participant.
3. Tell groups they have 1 minute to list 4 to 5 topics they would like to hear others' predictions about. (Examples include: healthcare, information technology, U.S. economy) Individuals should complete the sentences with these topics on a Predictions Activity Sheet.
4. Tell individuals to take 1 minute to write notes about their own predictions on the group topics on their sheets.

5. Tell participants they have 4 minutes to discuss topics, hearing predictions from each person who has one.

6. After 4 minutes, ask for topics from each group. If pertinent, share predictions between groups.

VARIATIONS

1. If all participants are from the same organization, ask them to make predictions about the future of the organization—future products, services, stability, etc.

2. Ask participants to discuss predictions they've heard, and support or refute those predictions.

TIPS

1. Always begin the activity by suggesting a prediction that people are aware of. For instance, in 1999 one may be making predictions about the Y2K problem.

2. Use this with a specific organization if the topic of the meeting is related to the future.

PREDICTIONS ACTIVITY SHEET

Please writes notes under each topic for which you would like to make predictions.

Topic: _____

My predictions:

_____

_____

_____

_____

_____

_____

Topic: _____

My predictions:

_____

_____

_____

_____

_____

_____

Topic: _____

My predictions:

_____

_____

_____

_____

_____

Topic: _____

My predictions:

_____
_____
_____
_____
_____
_____

Topic: _____

My predictions:

_____
_____
_____
_____
_____
_____

Topic: _____

My predictions:

_____
_____
_____
_____
_____
_____

62. LONGEST LIST

PURPOSE

Super Intelligent

GROUP SIZE

10 to 30

LEVEL OF PHYSICAL ACTIVITY

Medium

ESTIMATED TIME

5 to 6 minutes

PROPS

Longest List Activity Sheet, one per participant

This is a friendly competitive event. Groups will compete for the longest list as they create lists on the topic(s) provided.

INSTRUCTIONS

1. Organize participants into groups of two to six.
2. Explain that they will have a short competition to stimulate thinking.
3. Distribute one Longest List Activity Sheet to each person.
4. Tell them they have 3 minutes working in their groups to come up with the longest list. Explain that they should choose a recorder who will write the list quickly as group members speak out their responses.
5. At the end of three minutes, ask groups to count the numbers of items under each topic.

6. Select the group that generated the longest list and ask the group recorder to read each item on the list. Encourage the rest of the participants to listen for duplication or error.

7. Tell each group to report the number of items under each topic.

8. Encourage groups to report aloud the list from one topic.

VARIATIONS

1. Ask all groups to contribute one topic; then distribute all topics to each group.

2. Have a lottery to match a topic with a group, and have the group create the list aloud for all participants to hear.

TIPS

1. This needs to be kept light and moving quickly.

2. Have people stand while they think of items for the list. It helps with the energy flow.

Please list as many items as you can think of for each topic.

TOPIC 1: Times and Places You Have to Wait

TOPIC 2: Times and Places You Are Most Likely to Repeat Yourself

TOPIC 3: Times and Places You Are Most Likely to Laugh

63. ONE-LINERS

PURPOSE

Super Intelligent

GROUP SIZE

8 to 20

LEVEL OF PHYSICAL ACTIVITY

Low

ESTIMATED TIME

3 to 4 minutes

PROPS

None

In this fun activity, participants are encouraged to remember and to guess lines from books, movies or famous people.

INSTRUCTIONS

1. Organize participants into pairs.
2. Instruct each pair to come up with at least one famous line from a book, movie, or famous person that no one else will think of.
3. After one minute, explain that each pair will get to speak their line with appropriate inflections or intonations while the rest of the pairs have 20 seconds to write on a piece of paper where the line came from and who said it.

4. After each pair has spoken their lines, and participants have recorded responses, review correct answers with each pair repeating their lines and participants guessing the answer.

5. Determine the winner by asking which pair had the most correct answers.

VARIATIONS

1. Ask one pair at a time to share their lines before and after breaks, after lunch, etc.

2. Write down famous lines for yourself, and ask who said it, waiting for immediate response.

TIP

Encourage participants to think of as many lines as possible, and keep it going as long as you want.

64. TOOLS-FOR-THE-TRADE

PURPOSE

Super Intelligent

GROUP SIZE

6 to 20

LEVEL OF PHYSICAL ACTIVITY

Low

ESTIMATED TIME

3 to 4 minutes

PROPS

None

Participants will hear about tools others have found valuable, plus get to share their own experiences. Use this activity before introducing a tool they will be using on the job, or before asking them to create a tool to meet a specific need.

INSTRUCTIONS

1. Explain to participants that smarter people tend to find and use tools that give them the "cutting edge" at whatever task they're about.

2. Give them an example of a simple tool that has made a noticeable difference for you. (Examples may include a type of software or application, cooking utensil, or a handyman wonder.)

3. Ask participants to think of a tool that has made a significant difference to them and share them with the group.

4. Allow about 10 seconds per person (unless others express great interest).

VARIATIONS

1. Ask people to play act the using of the tool and ask other participants to guess.

2. Ask participants to "sell" this tool to others in the room. You might then ask who was the best salesperson.

TIPS

1. Although this is usually light, don't be surprised if someone brings up a tool used with a health problem.

2. Keep a record of these tools to include in a meeting summary. They'll appreciate it.

65. MERGERS AND ACQUISITIONS

PURPOSE

Super Intelligent

GROUP SIZE

8 to 30

LEVEL OF PHYSICAL ACTIVITY

Low

ESTIMATED TIME

4 to 6 minutes

PROPS

Mergers and Acquisitions Activity Sheet, one per participant

Many intelligent people are keeping track of business mergers and acquisitions. In this activity, participants will get to create different kinds of humorous mergers and acquisitions—kinds that have far fewer financial and personal repercussions.

INSTRUCTIONS

1. Organize participants into groups of 4 to 5.
2. Give each group a Mergers and Acquisitions Activity Sheet.
3. Tell participants they will have five minutes to create significant mergers and acquisitions by following the directions on the Activity Sheet.
4. After five minutes, ask groups to share their mergers and acquisitions.

VARIATIONS

1. Make this an individual activity.
2. Take it a step further, asking groups to create ad campaigns for at least one merger and one acquisition they've created.

TIP

You may extend this activity as far as you have time and ideas for.

MERGERS AND ACQUISITIONS ACTIVITY SHEET

In today's world, banks are merging and software developers are acquiring. Keeping with the times, create and name your own mergers and acquisitions for the following categories below.

Mergers

1. Businesses that don't usually go together

2. People that traditionally don't belong together

3. Governments of the world that don't seemingly belong together

Acquisitions

1. Businesses acquiring retail establishments that are totally unrelated

2. Businesses acquiring objects that are for employee use

3. Countries acquiring articles in space or under water that may be of use in the future

About the Author

Edie West is author of *201 Icebreakers*. She is currently executive director of the National Skill Standards Board in Washington, D.C. Prior to 1997, Edie's business was consulting, speaking, facilitating, and creating products for speakers and trainers.

Ms. West has a bachelor's degree in English from Eastern College, St. David's, Pennsylvania, and a master of education degree in Administration from the University of Vermont, Burlington, Vermont.

Edie loves to hear from icebreaker users and creators. You may converse with her by E-mail at ediewest@aol.com.